Black Hawk

and the Warrior's Path

American Biographical History Series

Black Hawk
and the Warrior's Path

Roger L. Nichols
University of Arizona

Harlan Davidson, Inc.
Arlington Heights, Illinos 60004

Copyright © 1992
Harlan Davidson, Inc.

Library of Congress Cataloging-in-Publication Data
Nichols, Roger L.
    Black hawk—and the warrior's path / Roger L. Nichols.
    p. cm.—(The American biographical history series)
Includes bibliographical references and index.
ISBN 0-88295-884-4
1. Black Hawk, Sauk chief, 1767–1838. 2. Sauk
Indians—Biography. 3. Black Hawk War. 1832. I. Title. II.
Series.
E83.83.B6N43 1992
973'.0497302—dc20
[B]   91-25985
                                                      CIP

Cover design: Roger Eggers
Cover illustration: Courtesy Library of Congress

Manufactured in the United States of America
96 95 94 93 92 1 2 3 4 5 MG

EDITORS' FOREWORD

As biographies offer access to the past, they reflect the needs of the present. Newcomers to biography and biographical history often puzzle over the plethora of books that some lives inspire. "Why do we need so many biographies of Abraham Lincoln?" they ask, as they search for the "correct" version of the sixteenth president's story. Each generation needs to revisit Lincoln because each generation has fresh questions, inspired by its own experiences. Collectively, the answers to these questions expand our understanding of Lincoln and America in the 1860s, but they also assist us to better comprehend our own time. People concerned with preserving such civil liberties as freedom of the press in time of national crisis have looked at Lincoln's approach to political opposition during and after secession. Civil rights activists concerned with racial injustice have turned to Lincoln's life to clarify unresolved social conflicts that persist more than a century after his assassination.

Useful as it is to revisit such lives, it is equally valuable to explore those often neglected by biographers. Almost always, biographies are written about prominent individuals who changed, in some measure, the world around them. But who is prominent and what constitutes noteworthy change are matters of debate. Historical beauty is definitely in the eye of the beholder. That most American biographies tell of great white males and their untainted accomplishments speaks volumes about the society that produced such uncritical paeans. More recently, women and men of various racial, religious, and economic backgrounds have expanded the range of American biography. The lives of prominent African-American leaders, Native American chieftains, and immigrant sweatshop workers who climbed the success ladder to its top now crowd onto those library shelves next to familiar figures.

In the American Biographical History Series, specialists in key areas of American History describe the lives of important men and women of many different races, religions, and ethnic backgrounds as those figures shaped and were shaped by the political, social, economic, and cultural issues of their day and the people with whom they lived. Biographical subjects and readers share a dialogue across time and space as biographers pose the questions suggested by life in modern-day America to those who lived in other eras. Each life offers a timeless reservoir of answers to questions from the present. The result is at once edifying and entertaining.

The concise biographical portrait found in each volume in this series is enriched and made especially instructive by the attention paid to generational context. Each biographer has taken pains to link his or her subject to peers and predecessors engaged in the same area of accomplishment. Even the rare individuals whose ideas or behavior transcend their age operated within a broad social context of values, attitudes, and beliefs. Iconoclastic radicals, too, whatever their era, owed a debt to earlier generations of protesters and left a legacy for those who would resist the status quo in the future.

Biographers in the series offer readers new companions, individuals of accomplishment, whose lives and works can be weighed and assessed and consulted as resources in answering the nagging questions that the thoughtful in every generation ask of the past to better comprehend the present. The makers of America—male and female, black and white and red and yellow, Christian, Moslem, Jew, atheist, agnostic, and polytheist, rich and poor and in between—all testify with their lives that the past is prologue. Anxious to share his rich experiences with those willing to listen, an elderly Eastern European immigrant living in Pittsburgh boasted, "By myself, I'm a book!" He, too, realized that an important past could be explicated through the narrative of a life, in fact, his own.

When a biographer sees his or her subject in broader context, important themes are crystallized, an era is illuminated. The single life becomes a window to a past age and its truths for succeeding generations and for you.

ALAN M. KRAUT
JON L. WAKELYN

To Martha C. Bernth

CONTENTS

PREFACE

During the past several decades Native American societies have gotten increased attention. As a result, today American Indian history flourishes as scholars and the reading public alike continue to view the story of tribal peoples as fascinating. Still, one hesitates to prepare a biography of an individual Indian unless that person is well known, and the life stories of most famous Native Americans are already in print. I was therefore delighted to be able to complete this study of Black Hawk for Harlan Davidson's New American Biographical History Series. Black Hawk has interested me for years, and completing this book has been more enjoyable than any other one I have had published.

Writing biography is always risky, but never more than when the subject is a person who left only a dim paper trail for the researcher to follow. Black Hawk made the job easier than many early Indian leaders would have by dictating his story to an Illinois newspaperman in 1833, and so both of them deserve as much thanks as anyone for this book coming into completion. In addition to those long-dead men of a century past, many others contributed to my success with this project. Professor Jon Wakelyn, one of the coeditors, asked me to contribute to the biography series and responded enthusiastically when I suggested writing about Black Hawk. He and coeditor Professor Alan Kraut read the manuscript and offered encouragement along the way. Professor R. David Edmunds critiqued the manuscript with a sharp eye, providing insightful comments once a draft had been prepared. Maureen Gilgore Hewitt and the rest of the Harlan Davidson staff offered suggestions and helped during the production phases of the book.

Others at several research institutions helped in the many ways they always do. In particular the staff of the Reader Services Division at the Library of Congress assisted by providing a comfortable place to write and to locate the many books, articles, and other materials that were necessary for my research. In past years staff people at the State Historical Society of Wisconsin and the Illinois State Historical Library offered invaluable help too. During 1990 the History Department of the University of Arizona gave me time away from my teaching duties so that I could finish the research for and prepare the manuscript that became this book. That same spring and summer the American Philosophical Society awarded me a grant that helped pay some of my travel and research costs. Two other people need recognition here. My wife, Marilyn J. Nichols, had the thankless task of reading the early draft of the manuscript and helped me avoid errors of both muddled logic and fractured syntax. Finally, Mary Sue Passe, the University of Arizona's history department manuscript secretary, prepared the final version of the manuscript with all her usual competence and cheerfulness. All of these people and institutions have my deepest appreciation.

ROGER L. NICHOLS
Tucson, Arizona

CHAPTER ONE

Who is Black Hawk?
1600–1804

General Edmund P. Gaines, a veteran frontier soldier, had issued the call for an urgent council. His orders directed him to move the troublesome segment of Sauk and Mesquakie Indians, known as the British Band, west across the Mississippi River into Iowa. As Gaines and his aides waited, Indian leaders arrived at the Rock Island agency house. Keokuk and Wapello, two of the principal chiefs, and their followers entered the meeting place, crowding it to the doors. Then Black Hawk and his partisans appeared. Armed with their lances, spears, and war clubs, and carrying their bows strung with arrows at the ready, they marched up to the door chanting a war song. Seeing that the supporters of his competitor Keokuk had already filled the room, Black Hawk refused to enter. Instead the taciturn warrior waited until General Gaines had ordered some of the others from the room. Then Black Hawk and a few of his adherents stalked into the chamber.

Gaines had remained seated until the latecomers filed in and then rose to address the tribal leaders. Although aware that some of his listeners carried more than the usual number of weapons into the council house, he had taken no notice except to increase the guard quietly. As he spoke the general reminded the Indians that nearly three decades earlier they had sold the land on which their major village stood and that they had signed several subsequent agreements with the United States recognizing the validity of that cession. He chided them for causing the expense of having to bring troops up the Mississippi River from Jefferson Barracks, near St. Louis, just to get them to do what they had already promised. Urging them to think of their own best interests by cooperating and keeping the peace, he encouraged the Indians to move west across the Mississippi immediately.

According to his own account, Black Hawk began speaking almost before the General could retake his seat. "We had never sold our country," he insisted. "We never received any annuities from our American father! And we are determined to hold onto our village."

Bolting to his feet, the angry Gaines demanded, "Who is Black Hawk? Who is Black Hawk?"

Just as quickly a flushed Black Hawk retorted, "I am a Sauk! My forefather was a SAUK! and all the Nations call me a SAUK!" With that exchange the council lost even the façade of civility. Bluntly, General Gaines gave the Indians two days to move west across the Mississippi, threatening to forcibly vacate them if they refused. To that the aging warrior responded that "I never could consent to leave my village," and he remarked that he was determined not to leave it. With those words, the meeting ended as the angry participants separated. During the next year, 1832, American forces destroyed the British Band, and incarcerated Black Hawk and the other Indian leaders in chains at Jefferson Barracks.

Black Hawk's shouted insistence on his identity as a Sauk provides the key to his years as a youth and young adult, as well as to his self-image and relationship to the Indian past. He grew to manhood at a time when traditional customs remained supreme. These included everything from the naming ceremony for a baby to the burial rites and mourning practices for the dead. Although clearly affected by long-time white presence in eastern North America, the Sauks and their close neighbors the Mesquakies had maintained rich cultural traditions and strong tribal identities down to the beginning of the nineteenth century. In the decades that followed the American War for

Independence, growing white influence and economic pressures buffeted many native groups, and the tribes of the Mississippi Valley could not avoid the turbulence that swirled around them.

These pressures came at the time young Black Hawk was growing to manhood, and they clearly upset him. Whether or not consciously aware that the changes resulted from white actions, the young Sauk increasingly saw himself as a defender of the village and tribal traditions. When his father died, Black Hawk proudly announced that he "now fell heir to the great medicine bag of my forefathers, which had belonged to my father." He stood then at a watershed in history for the Sauk and Mesquakie people. Fundamental changes in economics, diplomacy, and society swept across eastern North America as the British replaced the defeated French after 1763 and the British and Americans competed bitterly with each other after 1776. During those tumultuous decades, Black Hawk tended to look backward, to favor long-established traditions and practices rather than to accommodate the present. He had learned the lessons of his forefathers well. Unfortunately these lessons did not always fit the new situations he would face as a mature adult.

The almost willful self-destructiveness Black Hawk had displayed at the June 1831 meeting with General Gaines illustrated a long-demonstrated trait of the Sauk people. Since first encountering Europeans in the early seventeenth century, the actions taken by the Sauks and their allies the Mesquakies (or Foxes) appear to have been short-sighted, even ruinous. Nevertheless, their behavior resulted from well-thought-out motivations and clearly recognized principles of conduct. By the late eighteenth century the whites considered the Sauks and Mesquakies a single tribe. That was incorrect. Although related by language and culture, and enjoying substantial cooperation and even intermarriage, the two peoples always remained separate entities in their own minds.

The Osakiwugi or Sauks called themselves the yellow earth people, while their neighbors the Mesquakies were known as the red earth people. Both tribes spoke closely related language variations of what ethnologists call the Central Algonquian group, and during the late prehistoric era they used the technology of many eastern woodland peoples. They hunted, fished, gathered, and farmed as did their aboriginal neighbors. They erected permanent villages with multiple-family lodges built of poles, mats, and bark, living in them during the summer while their nearby crops matured. Their technology remained simple, based primarily on the use of wood, bone, and stone implements. They were adept at weaving mats, fashioning animal skins into clothing, and making earthenware pottery. Except when unusual weather, such as a severe winter or a particularly late spring, brought hardship, these people conducted their affairs in relative stability prior to the European invasion of North America. Thousands of foreigners came to the continent, and with them came disease, demands for land, and fundamental economic, political, and diplomatic changes in the tribes' relationships with each other.

Sauk traditions told of Black Hawk's great grandfather Na-na-ma-kee, or Thunder, meeting a French explorer, perhaps Samuel de Champlain, near present Montreal at the beginning of the seventeenth century. Increasing warfare with their Indian neighbors drove the Sauks westward from their probable home in southern Ontario, and a few decades later they lived in the Saginaw Bay area in eastern Michigan. From there they followed several other Central Algonquian peoples, including the Mesquakies, into western and southern Michigan and beyond into Wisconsin. By the period of the Iroquois wars, extending from the 1640s through the 1670s, other Indians fled before the ever-more-wide-ranging Iroquois war parties as the entire pattern of tribal locations underwent major disruptions. By the 1660s Jesuit missionaries reported that several of the Algonquian tribes had forced their way into the Green Bay region of eastern Wisconsin, an area formerly claimed almost exclusively by the Winnebago people. The Winnebagoes gave way grudgingly, but the invading groups remained small and there was plenty of land, with ample resources for the natives and the newcomers alike.

The Sauks migrated west to the shores of Green Bay, as did the Mesquakies, Potawatomis, and others. The new tribal homes, seemingly out of the reach of the dreaded Iroquois war parties, turned out to be good ones for the refugees. By the 1680s the Sauks and Mesquakies had erected their villages, cleared and cultivated land, and learned to exploit the local resources effectively. They became successful farmers quickly and soon sold their surplus corn and other foodstuffs to the French traders who traveled from Green Bay up the Fox River, down the Wisconsin, and west to the Mississippi and beyond in their neverending quest for furs. Clearly from their earliest contacts with the whites, these Indians had experienced frequent changes in their economic, social, and diplomatic/military relations with those around them. Driven from their eastern homes, and forced to invade the territory of other tribes, they learned to shift their allegiances and alter their economic practices to fit their new circumstances.

However, the immigrant tribes continued to face disruptions of their economies and societies as the pressures to find new sources of furs and the ongoing European imperial competition complicated life for all the peoples of eastern North America. The endemic warfare, trade, and diplomatic rivalries forced many Indian groups into several generations of changing locations. Certainly the Sauks experienced their share of resettling during the eighteenth century as they established new villages, abandoned others, and joined neighboring Algonquian groups in multitribal settlements in Wisconsin, Michigan, Illinois, and Iowa. For example, by 1711 the Sauks had villages at Green Bay, but at least some of them had moved to the St. Joseph River in southwestern Michigan to live among the Potawatomis and Kickapoos.

That same year, 1711, a large Mesquakie group moved east and attacked Detroit. This action disrupted the fur trade there, so French troops from the garrison led Huron and Ottawa warriors against the invaders. Having suffered several hundred fatalities, the Mesquakies fled back to Wisconsin, but the incident set off several decade-long "Fox Wars" between the French and the Mesquakies and their allies, who repeatedly attacked French traders trying to use the Fox-Wisconsin waterway. Between 1719 and 1726, warriors from the Sauk, Mascouten, Kickapoo, and even Dakota Sioux joined in raids against the French. The Europeans arranged a peace in 1726, but just a year later renewed Mesquakie raids against the Illinois tribes and threats to divert the furs coming from Wisconsin and Illinois to the English enraged French officials. Hoping to end this disruption of their trade, the French launched what they assumed would be a final war to exterminate the tribe. For the next ten years invading forces of French and their Indian allies ravaged the Mesquakie settlements, destroying crops, burning villages, and killing as many people as possible.

For some years the Sauks aided the French in this war, but during the mid-1730s they joined their Mesquakie neighbors in raiding south into Illinois as well as in their defense against the French. Gradually members of the two tribes intermarried and moved into each others' villages. By 1730 some of the Sauks had joined the earlier migrants who had settled along the St. Joseph River. Other Sauks remained and that same year joined the Mesquakies in a major attack on the nearby Winnebagoes. Enemy raids continued as well, and in 1731, 1732, and 1733, bands of Hurons, Ottawas, Potawatomis, and Illinois warriors destroyed most of the Mesquakies and killed many Sauks too. These raids so weakened the Mesquakies that they fled to the Sauk villages for protection. Both peoples then retreated west to the Mississippi River and even beyond to escape their enemies.

Their migrations shifted the center of Sauk population south and gradually west, away from Green Bay and toward the Mississippi. The Mesquakies established new villages on the lower reaches of the Wisconsin River and south along the Mississippi from there. The Sauks settled near the mouth of the Rock River at present Rock Island, Illinois, as well as in eastern Iowa and at

Prairie du Sauk in southern Wisconsin for much of the rest of the century. Even during this confused era of repeated warfare and migration, Indian trade with the French at Green Bay and in central Illinois continued. Although ethnologists differ over the founding of what became Saukenuk, the principal tribal village, by the late 1730s some Sauks lived in its vicinity. It was there that Black Hawk was born in 1767, and the village remained at the center of his experiences and personal identification as a Sauk.

As an old man, Black Hawk recalled days of peace and plenty while he grew to adulthood. The village stood on the north side of the Rock River, just below the rapids, and on a broad point of land between that stream and the Mississippi. A rich prairie stretched from the front of the village to the larger river, while behind the village a bluff, extended gradually in the other direction. On the gently sloping land near the bluff, the Sauk women cultivated some eight hundred acres of fertile fields where they raised large crops of corn, beans, pumpkins, and squash. A heavy mat of bluegrass covered the uncultivated area nearby, and the villagers pastured several hundred horses there. Local springs provided good water, while the Rock River rapids proved an excellent spot for fishing. In the village itself, the Indians lived in large, permanent lodges built of poles, with bark and mats for the sides and roofs. Saukenuk, with up to several thousand residents and at least a hundred lodges, had become the center of tribal activity by the end of the eighteenth century.

From there, and smaller villages like it, Sauk warriors crisscrossed parts of eastern Iowa, northern Illinois, and southern and central Wisconsin as they hunted and raided. Despite their hatred of the French, which grew out of the Fox Wars, the Sauks liked the British little better at first, and they joined Pontiac's Rebellion against them. The Sauk's first hostile actions toward the British came at Michilimackinac, where they played lacrosse with the local Ojibwas outside the gates of the British fort. While the men played ball, the Indian women slipped into the fort, carrying weapons hidden under their loosely worn blan-

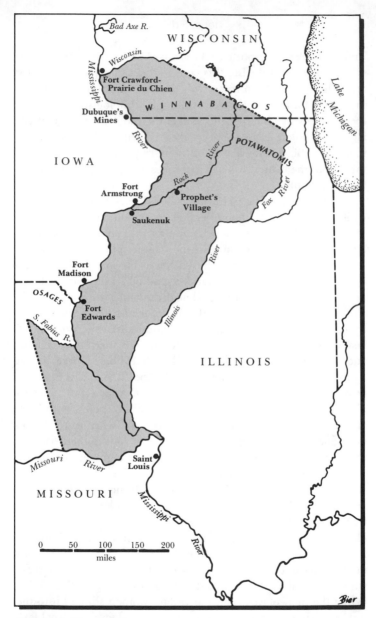

The Sauk Homeland

kets. At an agreed upon time in the game, one of the Indians threw the ball over the wall and the braves rushed through the open gate and into the garrison, ostensibly to retrieve the lost ball. When the warriors entered the fort they ignored the errant ball, grabbed their weapons, and, before the soldiers realized what had happened, captured the entire garrison. It remains unclear how much of the fighting they did that summer day, or if they participated at all, but it does seem unlikely that Sauk warriors, who prized military honors highly, would have stayed away from the fight.

War parties left Saukenuk and other villages to do battle with Indian foes, too, as the tribe considered a host of other native peoples its enemies. To the south they raided the Kaskaskias and Cherokees, while beyond the Mississippi they attacked the Pawnees occasionally and the Osages frequently.

Many factors caused these intermittent conflicts, including: Sauk ideas about honor for successful warriors; a fairly loose tribal and village political structure; and religious-social beliefs about individual fasting and visions. Tribal government included both peace and war chiefs. The tribal council represented twelve clans or sibs within the Sauk nation with each one having at least one member to represent it. Operating alongside this "formal" structure were village or band leaders who had no official standing as chiefs. For example, neither Black Hawk nor Keokuk, his main rival, held the rank of civil chief despite their prominence in tribal affairs. Although not supreme, the tribal council exercised considerable authority, particularly when dealing with other Indians, the Europeans, or, later, the United States.

Often the tribal council sought to oversee interracial meetings with traders, soldiers, or government officials. Once the Sauk lands became a part of the United States, the council participated in negotiations with the government on issues including states of war, trade alliances, and land cessions. When considering significant matters, the council included at least a representative sample of the tribal or village population, including the warriors, women, and even children. In this way major decisions had at least some participation from tribal members who could then spread knowledge of the council's actions. Thus, this system of government worked more often through persuasion and social pressure than physical or economic coercion. The villages had no police to enforce agreements, and when tribal members objected strongly to council decisions they were always free to leave for another village. This option kept public debate to a minimum, but it meant that the fabric of tribal life might be rent at any time by major disputes that could not be settled by persuasion.

While the Sauk chiefs and their tribal council directed civil intra- and intertribal relations, their authority did not extend to decisions regarding the initiation or execution of war; because of the modest social controls civil leaders exercised over individual warriors, conflict remained endemic for generations.

Wars began in different ways. Occasionally the tribal council received emissaries from other tribes who carried wampum belts, asking the Sauks to join them in a war against a particular enemy. Generally the enemies were other Indian groups or one or more of the competing European imperial powers, and the resulting conflicts often lasted several years or more.

The most frequent warfare, however, consisted of scattered or even isolated raids against traditional enemies such as the Sioux, Osages, or Cherokees. Far more common than major wars, these raids resulted from the actions of single individuals. If anyone killed or injured an individual Sauk, custom demanded a response. Even such things as personal insults or dreams of injury or death might set the war machinery in motion. If the incident occurred within the village or involved people considered to be allies, the band leaders usually could prevent violent retaliation by getting the family responsible for the injury to offer gifts to the victim's family "to cover the blood," as they described the process. However, if a member of another tribe, particularly a traditional rival or enemy, proved to be responsible for the incident, tribal custom required the adult males of the affected family to seek revenge. Although the family members needed some public support, the process for organizing a war party remained relatively simple. A respected warrior in the family announced that he would be leading a war party in response to the offending incident or dream and asked for help. Volunteers, often young men eagerly seeking war honors, agreed to follow the leader's direction. Even when the tribal council objected to a raid, the participants individually fasted and prayed to purify themselves. To be at full strength for their venture, prior to leaving the village the warriors held a sacred ceremony seeking spiritual power. If the raid was successful, they returned to report victory, bringing captives and scalps for a celebration in their home village. Casualties and fatalities of their own brought mourning at the same time. Unfortunately, each time Sauk warriors triumphed over their enemies, the other tribe felt honor-bound to retaliate, and so a cycle of raids and counter-raids developed, making intertribal peace almost impossible to achieve.

Sauk and Mesquakie economic practices further complicated a peaceful existence for the groups. Frequent movements of the villagers were required throughout the year. Each spring the people returned to their permanent villages where they opened the caches of food stored the preceding autumn, repaired the lodges, cleared the weeds from the fields, planted their crops, and then held their annual medicine feast, or feast of the dead. Black Hawk recalled that during the early summer the villagers held what he called "our national dance." This ceremony honored the successful hunters and warriors and helped fuel the desires of the boys and young men hoping to gain fame as noted warriors. With the entire village participating, the chiefs and headmen sat at one end of the dance area while the drummers and singers remained at the other end. The men lined one side of the square while the women stood across from them. Then the warriors entered the square individually, each one recounting his actions in past warfare to the applause of the villagers. The young men and teenage boys who lacked warrior status

could only stand on the edges of the gathering; they were not allowed to enter the ceremonial square. As a young boy Black
Hawk felt "ashamed to look where our young women stood, before I could take my stand in the square as a warrior."

When the ceremonies ended, the cropland had been prepared, and the corn stood about knee-high, most of the adult
men rode west to hunt buffalo on the plains. During the summer hunt the Sauks often collided with similar parties of Sioux
or Pawnees as each group strove to claim the best hunting
grounds. Thus the hunts often increased intertribal violence
and warfare. With most of the young men away, the remaining
villagers split their tasks. Some traveled north to the lead-
mining region between Galena (Illinois) and the Dubuque
mines (near present Dubuque, Iowa) where they spent about six
weeks of the summer digging and smelting lead to sell to their
traders later in the year. Those remaining in the village spent
their time fishing in the Rock River and gathering reeds from
which they made mats.

The various groups all returned to Saukenuk during August,
or the Moon of the Elk, when they exchanged meat, hides, lead,
dried fish, and mats. Black Hawk remembered the late summer
as the best time of the year, as the villagers feasted and enjoyed
good weather and plenty of food. When time came for the corn
harvest, the Sauks held a big celebration with dancing, feasting,
ball games, horse races, and gambling. Then they awaited the
arrival of their traders. The whites brought much-wanted hunting, trapping, and household goods, as well as cloth and blankets that the Indians needed in the winter. During the autumn
and winter the villagers broke into small hunting groups as they
crossed the Mississippi again in search of game. As winter
ended, they headed back to the maple groves to make sugar and
hunted the numerous waterfowl then migrating back north.
Then they returned to the village to start the annual cycle anew.

Little is known of Black Hawk's family or childhood, although scraps of information suggest little about the youngster
that would have been unusual for a Sauk boy at the time. A

member of the Eagle Clan, Pyesa, his father, claimed to be the grandson of Na-na-ma-kee. Of the boy's mother, Kneebingke-mewoin, or Summer Rain, even less is known. Black Hawk had one younger brother, but it is not clear if he had any other brothers or sisters, if he did they left no marks on the historical record. At his baby-naming ceremony his father chose to call him Ma-ka-tai-me-she-kia-kiak or Black Sparrow Hawk, rather a long name for such a small person. As an adult he was known as Black Hawk, perhaps because of the Sauk custom of allowing warriors to modify or entirely change their names after display-ing some heroics in battles.

Living at Saukenuk, the youngster experienced the seasonal moves of the villagers as they hunted, farmed, fished, trapped, mined lead, and gathered sap (for maple sugar) each year. He saw the villagers deal with Spanish, French, British, and Ameri-can traders, and must have heard talk of wars between compet-ing groups of whites. During the American War for Inde-pendence, he learned first-hand of the results of dealing with the whites. In the spring of 1780, British officials gathered a force of Winnebago, Sauk, Mesquakie, and Menominee warriors in southern Wisconsin and then set off down the Wisconsin and Mississippi rivers to attack the Spanish settlement at St. Louis and the French community of Cahokia, just across the river in Illinois. This force of some 950 Indians and traders passed Saukenuk on its way south. It is not possible to know how many Sauk warriors from the village joined this force, but by late May the raiders reached their destination. On May 26 the British and Indian force attacked St. Louis but failed to overrun the town. Their attack at Cahokia also failed, although both communities suffered casualties.

The British thrust in the Mississippi Valley caused George Rogers Clark, the tough Virginian then commanding American forces in Illinois, to strike back immediately. He gathered a force of some 350 American troops, French militiamen, and Spanish civilians from the nearby towns and under the com-mand of Colonel John Montgomery sent them after the retreating enemy. The small army moved up the Illinois River by boat as far as Peoria, but their foes eluded them. Then Montgomery led his troops northwest to the Rock River, where they hoped to attack the Sauks and Mesquakies. However, scouts from the villages alerted the Indians well before the attackers arrived, so the Sauks and their neighbors fled. Angry at having missed their quarry, the whites burned Saukenuk and the nearby villages to the ground. Fortunately for the Indians, the early June attack meant that some of their crops probably survived.

A rumor suggests that Black Hawk's mother, Summer Rain, too sick to travel when the villagers left, died in the flames of the burning lodges. That was highly unlikely because the family would have moved her to safety by canoe or horse-drawn travois. Whatever the case, the June 1780 destruction of the village may well have been the youngster's first personal experience with Americans. He gave no indication of his reactions upon returning to help rebuild the village he had known as home from his earliest memories; still it seems likely that the impressionable youth could not escape feeling a strong hatred toward Americans for a time.

Within the next couple of years the young teenager's life would change drastically. At age fifteen, Black Hawk accompanied a war party, and during the melee of battle he wounded one of the enemy. This did not bring him the coveted status of warrior, but when emissaries from the Mascouten tribe visited Saukenuk recruiting warriors for a raid against the Osages, Pyesa and his son volunteered. Eager to prove his bravery to his father, Black Hawk killed one of the Osages. After tearing off the victim's scalp, he ran to show Pyesa his trophy. His father "said nothing, but looked pleased," Black Hawk reported fondly years later.

Killing the Osage warrior proved to be a pivotal experience in the teenager's life. The victorious war party hurried home with scalps to display and stories of valor and excitement to share. At Saukenuk the warriors chanted their victory songs as they marched proudly into the town. That evening Black Hawk took part in his first scalp dance, a high point in the life of any young Sauk male. While the entire village watched expectantly, each warrior danced individually, chanting a description of his actions in the battle. Those few who actually returned with enemy scalps received special recognition and applause from the gathering. Having proven himself as a warrior, Black Hawk not only participated in the scalp dance for the first time, but he received the coveted feather that only recognized, experienced braves could wear. Of equal importance, his accomplishment showed that his medicine (spiritual power) was strong, and should he choose to lead a war party in the future others might well follow his lead despite his youth.

A few months later the newly minted warrior decided to launch an attack against the Osages beyond the Mississippi. Announcing his intention, he built a separate, small lodge at the edge of the village and prepared pipes, tobacco, and red cloth for his visitors. Then he waited for some of the other young, restless men of the village to respond. To each man who entered he offered a pipe, and when they had smoked he discussed his plans. Then he offered a strip of red cloth to those who seemed likely to participate in his raid. The volunteers took the cloth, running it through their hand to signify that they would join him and accept his leadership. Seven others agreed to follow his lead, and after the proper ceremonies he rode west ahead of the small band of warriors. Some days later the Sauks encountered a party of one hundred Osages. After killing one of them, Black Hawk decided that the Osage party was too large and well-armed for his small group, so he led his men safely back to Saukenuk.

Even this minor foray brought additional recognition of his skills as a leader. Because Black Hawk won "great applause" and increased stature as a young warrior from this incident, a few months later when he proposed another attack on the Osages, some 180 braves responded to his call. The war party moved across the countryside without incident, but when it reached the Osage village, the young partisan led his men into an empty camp. Their enemies had fled. For most of the Sauks this occurrence indicated a weakness in Black Hawk's medicine, so the disappointed warriors abandoned their now discredited leader. Only five men chose to remain, and together they set off after the Osages, hoping to kill or capture some stragglers. A few days later they killed an Osage man and boy, and, after taking their victims' scalps, hurried back to Saukenuk.

News of Black Hawk's failure cooled the braves' willingness to accept his calls for other attacks, so for the next several years he could not attract any followers. During that time he claimed that the Osages retaliated for his and earlier raids, "committing many outrages on our nation and people." Eventually, these attacks persuaded the Sauks that they needed revenge, so at age nineteen Black Hawk tried again. This time he led two hundred warriors. In a few days they met an Osage party of about equal size, and a pitched battle ensued. "Each party fought desperately," Black Hawk reported. "The enemy seemed unwilling to yield the ground, and we were determined to conquer or die!" The Sauks proved to be the more resolute and, by their count, killed nearly one hundred enemy warriors while losing only nineteen of their own. Black Hawk himself claimed to have killed five men and one woman during the battle, and he carried five scalps home in triumph.

This one-sided defeat by the Sauks persuaded the Osages to break off the war for the next several years. Without an obvious opponent, Black Hawk sought another target for tribal aggression. After a short time he called for an attack on the Cherokees because, he claimed, they "had decoyed and murdered some of our helpless children." Black Hawk's narrative fails to identify these people further, so it is not possible to know where they lived or how they became enemies to the Sauks. It is likely that the Cherokees he encountered were descendants of the Chickamauga band that had been defeated and scattered by pioneer militiamen, during the American Revolution, and who then fled west out of central Tennessee. The Cherokees posed a formidable risk, having many more warriors than all of the Sauk villages could muster. Only a few warriors accepted the call to arms, and Pyesa assumed command. He led the attackers south to the Meramec River just, a few miles south of St. Louis, where they encountered a larger group of Cherokees. Badly outnumbered, the Sauks fought desperately until their enemies retreated, leaving behind twenty-eight of their own men dead on the battlefield.

Although the Sauks seized a victory from this near disaster, the battle marked another important change for Black Hawk. Early in the fighting, Pyesa suffered a serious wound in his thigh, and when the battle ended, Black Hawk hurried back to his father only to learn from a medicine man that Pyesa was dying. Pyesa's father had been a medicine man and had kept the "great medicine bag" of the tribe. Upon his father's death, Black Hawk took possession of the bundle, although he never mentioned using it to exercise any sort of religious ceremonial role. Hurriedly burying their dead companions, the warriors returned to Saukenuk to perform their scalp dance and then to mourn their lost comrades. The young Sauk felt his father's death keenly, and Black Hawk entered a period of almost five years of deep mourning. Blackening his face, as was customary, he neglected his appearance, wearing only minimal and dirty clothing, fasting, and praying. An ultratraditionalist, he continued this regimen for five years, far beyond the usual six-month period of mourning. During that entire time he avoided the warpath, focusing his energies on hunting and fishing.

When Black Hawk resumed normal activities he did so as a mature warrior, aged twenty-four or five. He stood about five feet ten inches tall and had a medium build with broad shoulders and slender arms and legs. Like most Sauk men he had plucked his face and most of his head clean. At times he allowed slight eyebrows to grow, but at others he plucked these bare too. Atop his head he wore the traditional Sauk scalp lock to which he sometimes attached a tall roach of animal fur. Described as having a high forehead, an aquiline or Roman nose, a full mouth, a sharp and slightly receding chin, and a bright, direct gaze, he appeared stern—even dour—to the whites. Frequently, at least on ceremonial occasions, he carried the skin of a hawk, using its tail feathers as a fan.

When he returned to the warpath during the mid-1790s, Black Hawk turned his attention back to the hated Osages. He claimed that they had renewed their raids and attacks, so he led a small force against them. When his warriors encountered only a few of the enemy, he decided to capture them and turn them over to the Spanish authorities in St. Louis. Shortly after his return to Saukenuk, Black Hawk recruited one of the largest war parties he ever led. Reportedly including five hundred Sauks and Mesquakies as well as another one hundred Iowa braves, the group set out for the Osage country. After some days of travel they discovered an Osage village of forty lodges and, attacking at dawn the next day, destroyed the camp and all but two of its inhabitants. Claiming that his men killed many of the bravest Osage warriors, Black Hawk later reported that this defeat persuaded the Osages to remain at peace and away from Sauk hunting grounds for a time.

In the years just after 1800, Black Hawk participated in the frequent raids that constituted a central part of tribal life at the time. He wanted to avenge his father's death at the hands of the Cherokees but never succeeded in raising a large enough group of warriors to accomplish that feat. At age thirty-five he led yet another big war party, this time against a combination of the Ottawa, Kaskaskia, and Osage tribes. This became a long and difficult campaign during which the Sauks fought seven major battles and a number of minor skirmishes as well. By his account the enemy suffered several hundred fatalities, and he claimed to have "killed thirteen of their bravest warriors, with my own hand." Returning to Saukenuk to celebrate their victories, the warriors mourned their dead before settling back into their annual economic pattern.

Undoubtedly this narration of Black Hawk's early life omits much that would help to understand his later attitudes and actions, but several clear indications of his personality and world view do emerge. He thought of himself as a traditional Sauk. He personified tribal rivalries throughout much of his life. Thus, because the Osages had been long-time enemies of the tribe they became his enemies. He practiced the ceremonies, dances, and mourning customs with determination, often going far beyond minimal expectations, as in mourning his father for five years instead of the usual six months. He grew to manhood during an era when the Sauks and their tribal neighbors still enjoyed a good degree of isolation and freedom from the demands of the European powers then trying to divide the continent among themselves.

At the same time, the effects of European-Indian diplomacy, an ever-expanding fur trade, and the steady growth of the white population were beginning to place crippling restraints on Indian freedom of action. While the villagers might cross to the west side of the Mississippi to hunt and raid, growing numbers of white settlements limited their travels, hunting, or war-making to the east. Even more significant, as the white settlements grew so did pressure on the Indians to sell some or all of their land and move west. By the dawn of the nineteenth century, the Sauks and Mesquakies encountered more difficulties in hunting and trapping, because whenever they left the immediate vicinity of their summer villages they chanced meeting hunting or war parties of Osages, Pawnees, or Sioux. Thus they found themselves being squeezed between the whites on the east and their traditional rivals and enemies on the west, meanwhile hunting for diminished numbers of game animals and growing ever more dependent on the fur trade to provide them with the manufactured goods they had come to accept and rely upon. Occasionally, unscrupulous traders cheated Indian hunters out of their furs with alcohol, which also caused brawls and injuries.

For Black Hawk and his fellow Sauk and Mesquakie tribesmen, the quality of life deteriorated steadily. By 1800 he had become a mature warrior. He stood accepted as one of the Sauks' premier war leaders, a veteran of many campaigns, and a participant in the burial ceremonies, scalp dances, and other tradi-

tional practices in Saukenuk. His entire life to that moment
pointed back—back to a time when the Indians had enjoyed the
freedom to migrate, hunt, make war, or conduct diplomacy with
little interference from the whites. Had he been asked the question in 1800 that General Gaines raised rhetorically in 1831, his
answer might well have been the same. "I am a Sauk!"

CHAPTER TWO

The Americans were coming to take possession ♦ 1803–16

In March 1804, Black Hawk and a small group of warriors traveled to St. Louis to see the man they called their Spanish father. Charles Dehault Delassus, the Spanish governor of upper Louisiana since 1799, had gained the Sauks' trust and friendship. In fact, they had turned prisoners over to him several times and enjoyed his hospitality. When the Indians reached the town, they dragged their canoes from the river, put up temporary lodges, and prepared to meet the governor. After painting their faces carefully and arranging their clothing to their satisfaction, they strode through the motley crowd at the waterfront. Noticing that some of the townspeople appeared troubled, Black Hawk asked what had happened. The answer confounded him. We learned "that the Americans were coming to take possession of the town and country," he reported, "and that we should lose our Spanish father!" Expressing sorrow at losing their friendly trade and contacts with the Spanish, he contrasted this positive relationship with the "bad accounts of the Americans" the Sauks had received from tribal groups living near them.

The Indians stayed in town for several more days and on March 9, 1804, the actual transfer of sovereignty took place. Captain Amos Stoddard of the U.S. Army took possession of

Louisiana from Delassus, who acted as France's representative. The next day, American control replaced that of France, while Black Hawk and his companions witnessed the proceedings with some apprehension. When Captain Stoddard arrived at the Spanish governor's home, the Sauks had just finished their last visit with the Spaniard. As Stoddard came to one door of the building the Indians slipped out another and set off for their canoes on the riverbank. The Sauks lost no time in expressing their discontent with the idea of having the Americans as neighbors on both sides of the Mississippi. As a result, by early summer 1804 Stoddard complained that "The Saucks...certainly do not pay that respect to the United States which is entertained by the other Indians—and in some instances they have assumed a pretty elevated tone" toward the Americans.

The modest ceremony in the muddy downtown streets of St. Louis brought permanent changes to Indian-white relations in the upper Mississippi Valley region. Not only had the United States obtained the landrights to a region that stretched west to the Rocky Mountains, but, with so much open land beyond the Mississippi, the government was becoming more receptive to the pioneers' demands that tribes living around the Great Lakes and along the Ohio and Mississippi rivers be moved west. For the Indians of Illinois, Wisconsin, Missouri, Iowa, and Minnesota, American acquisition of Louisiana was to lead to their first extensive contact with the expanding American society and its government. Having dealt with the French, British, and Spanish previously, and being firmly enmeshed in the fur trade system, the tribes had plenty of experience with whites. Nevertheless, the Americans' entry into the region altered Indian-white relations fundamentally. Previously, the Europeans had come into the region in small numbers, and they had striven to keep the tribes happy by giving them presents and conducting a healthy trade. Some Americans wanted this system to continue, but most wanted only one thing—Indian land. Thus, whites, who had been seen as generally friendly, soon became feared enemies with the power to destroy the existing structures of tribal society.

Beginning on a slightly sour note in 1804, relations between the Sauks and Mesquakies and the Americans remained strained, as the newcomers soon took steps to fulfill Black Hawk's prediction about their taking Indian lands. The Sauk villagers had considered the now-departed Spanish their friends who had favored them over their hated enemies, the Osages. The Americans, however, behaved in an opposite manner. In fact, the U.S. officials had orders to be "particularly attentive" to the Osages and had given them a great number of presents since taking charge in St. Louis. Furthermore, the Sauks thought that the United States had not dealt honestly with them the year before when it had purchased lands from the Kaskaskia tribe south of the Illinois River. Both the Sauk and Kickapoo tribes had at least a claim to some of that region, and the American negotiators had ignored both groups during the purchase talks. Nevertheless, the Sauk's long-term war against the Osages remained the crucial issue in their early relations with the United States, particularly when they thought that the Americans tended to favor their enemies. When U.S. officials intercepted and turned back a three-hundred-man war party headed for Osage country, Sauk and Mesquakie warriors seethed with outrage. This was another manifestation of the intruders' siding with their enemies! At the same time, the presence of small groups of American pioneers squatting illegally on tribal hunting lands along the Quivre River, just north of St. Louis, confirmed the Indians' suspicions that the Americans intended to join with the Osages to cut off the Sauks and Mesquakies from their southern hunting territory.

The situation looked equally unsettled and dangerous from the Americans' vantage point. Together the Sauks and Mesquakies constituted one of the largest Indian groups in the area that had not concluded a peace treaty with the United States. They held Osage and other Indian prisoners whom they refused

to either release or surrender to American authorities. In addition, rumors reached St. Louis that the Sauk and Mesquakie leaders had sent "a speech with wampum" to the Kickapoos, asking that tribe to join them in a war against the pioneers, who were already filtering into Illinois. A Kickapoo observer reported that the Sauk emissaries rode around their village dragging an American flag from the tail of one of their horses. At this point both the Indians and the whites feared and perhaps even expected a war, and American officials even admitted that they had failed to deal even-handedly with the Sauks and the Osages.

Despite the tension and continuing misunderstanding between the Sauk and Mesquakie Indians and the Americans, both sides had reasons to seek peace. Federal officials from the president on down all realized that Indian wars, even short ones, proved to be enormous strains on the modest national budget. Peace and amicable trade relations were cheaper than war, but more important, they created a situation in which the Indians might be induced to sell their lands to the government (to make room for the continuing flood of pioneers surging west). The Indians, at the same time, depended on the whites for trade goods, and in order to exchange their furs, hides, lead, and even surplus food crops they had to maintain good relations with the Americans. The task facing the village leaders and the tribal councils, then, was how to keep trade links open while at the same time managing to salve tribal honor enough to dissuade the eager young men from taking to the warpath.

This dilemma caused Sauk leaders to protest to Stoddard, now the acting governor of Louisiana, about American actions that favored the Osages at the expense of the Sauks. They also asked that a government factory or trading post be located on their lands. At the same time, the Sauk's refusal to surrender an Osage prisoner held by the tribe angered Stoddard, so he made no effort to comply with their requests or to respond to their complaints about pioneers taking up claims on prime Sauk and Mesquakie hunting land. This mutual lack of trust soon

brought violence, as young Sauk warriors began raiding frontier settlements. In early autumn 1804, four Sauk warriors attacked one of the Quivre River settlements, killing three people "in a most barbarous manner," and leaving the corpses "with their scalps taken off."

The raid intensified matters. Something had to be done to pacify the frontier. The young men who had killed and scalped the pioneers rode back to their village, where they threw the grisly trophies on the ground in front of the chiefs and taunted them to "go cry with the whites." Sauk leaders acted quickly. Rightly fearing white retaliation, they moved four of their small villages north beyond the Des Moines River to get the women and children to safety. Then two Sauk chiefs and a trustworthy fur trader hurried to St. Louis hoping to defuse the situation. When they arrived, they admitted that some of the young warriors had committed the murders and offered to "cover the blood" of the victims by giving presents to the families of the deceased, as was the tribal custom. To their dismay, the Indians learned that the pioneers would accept no payment. Even then outraged settlers wanted to attack the nearby tribal villages and were gathering arms for retaliatory raids. It was only "with great difficulty, and upon promises of ample justice" that local officials dissuaded the vengeful whites.

After they admitted that their warriors had committed the killings, the chiefs went on to explain that they could not promise to surrender the young men to the whites. They explained truthfully that within the Sauk village society, chiefs lacked the coercive powers that white authorities had over the settlers. However, American officials refused to believe this, and Major James Bruff, then commanding the U.S. troops at St. Louis, demanded that the two chiefs return with the guilty men as soon as possible. If the Indians failed to comply, he feared that the frontier would remain "harassed by Murders and Robberies." Bruff also invited tribal leaders to meet William Henry Harrison, then territorial governor of Indiana, who would be in St. Louis later that fall to negotiate treaties with the tribes of the region.

The major hoped that the governor and the Indians might agree on how to settle the issue of the murders.

When the chiefs left St. Louis, they hurried north to consult leaders of the various Sauk villages. The tribal council decided to send a small delegation composed of minor village chiefs to settle matters with the Americans and avoid a war. Five men led by Quashquame and Pashipaho took one of the guilty young men along with them on their trip to St. Louis. There the whites imprisoned the young warrior; the chiefs then saw their task as gaining his release and keeping peace. Harrison seized the issue as a chance to achieve his unstated goal—to obtain a land cession from the Sauk and Mesquakie tribes. He kept no journal of the meetings, and the Indian participants either could not or would not recall just what happened, but when the talks ended the chiefs thought that they had secured their fellow tribesman's freedom by signing the papers Harrison placed before them.

The rest of the tribe wanted to know whether there was to be peace or war and awaited their return anxiously. Relatives of the young man in prison feared the worst. Some blackened their faces in mourning and anger, while others fasted in an effort to gain favorable treatment from the spirits. When the delegation returned by mid-November, they halted a short distance from Saukenuk to camp. There Black Hawk recalled that "they appeared to be dressed in fine coats, and had medals! From these circumstances, we were in hopes that they brought good news." Instead the news proved to be all bad. During their talks with Governor Harrison, Quashquame and his companions urged him to release the prisoner, but the governor wanted them to agree to a land cession. The Indians had little concept of formal treaties or of the whites' ideas about land ownership and seem to have understood that they were accepting general American sovereignty over the region in exchange for the release of the prisoner. When the talks ended, Quashquame and the others had failed to gain the release of their kinsman, who remained in jail at St. Louis. Although eventually pardoned by President Thomas Jefferson, the young Sauk never learned of his good fortune because he died the following spring from a gunshot wound while trying to escape from prison. Not only did the 1804 Sauk delegation fail to obtain the prisoner's freedom, but far worse, it wound up selling all of the tribal land east of the Mississippi.

The treaty of 1804, concluded in secret with a handful of minor chiefs not authorized to make such an agreement, and who later claimed that they had been kept drunk throughout much of their visit, remained at the root of nearly all later difficulties between the Sauks and Mesquakies and the United States. Quashquame and the other delegates to St. Louis had no authority to discuss anything except a settlement of the murders of the three whites on the Quivre River. The treaty itself gained at least one objective tribal leaders had sought. In becoming allies of the United States the Sauks and Mesquakies achieved a status on par with that of the Osage tribe. However, in addition the treaty: established machinery to settle future disputes between the two peoples; regularized future trade relations; spelled out the area of tribal lands and the conditions under which Indians would continue to enjoy their use; called for negotiations for a general peace between the Sauks, Mesquakies, and Osages; ceded all their lands east of the Mississippi and a small portion in Missouri; and provided the Indians a one-time payment of $2,234.50 and an annuity of $1,000.

Regardless of what the American officials at St. Louis might have told the tribal delegation, the Indians had no understanding of what they had done. The treaty ceded all Sauk and Mesquakie lands in Illinois and southern Wisconsin. It even included lands to which neither of the two tribes had any valid claim. The signers, certainly uninformed and possibly frightened as well as drunk, had no experience with such agreements. Their previous dealings with French, British, and Spanish authorities had never included any cession of territory. In fact, given their ideas and practices about land use, it is not clear that they even understood the whites' concept of land titles. What seems most likely is that the treaty signatories thought they had succeeded in heading off a potential war by signing a general agreement allying them with the United States, opening trade relations with the Americans, and providing a method to settle frontier difficulties. Apparently they thought they had acknowledged general American control of the region in a manner similar to the way they had responded to earlier French, British, or Spanish claims. Even had the negotiators been frightened for their lives, the chance that they would sell the lands that had been occupied by their largest villages for decades appears most unlikely. Their circumstances in 1804 simply made concessions of that sort unthinkable.

Whatever the truth about the treaty signing and what the Indians did or did not understand, the agreement proved extraordinarily one-sided and confusing. Despite repeated efforts to clarify their understanding of its terms, the Indians thought that Article Seven guaranteed their right to remain on their lands. That paragraph stated that "as long as the lands which are now ceded to the United States remain their property, the Indians belonging to the said tribes, shall enjoy the privilege of living and hunting upon them." For years Black Hawk maintained that the Sauks and Mesquakies understood this to mean that as long as the region remained a part of the United States the Indians could use it. When told that this was incorrect, he shifted to a narrower interpretation, one that guaranteed the Sauks their land until individual settlers purchased it from the government. This latter issue became the bone of contention during the 1828–31 era, when continuing incidents between illegal squatters and the villagers at Saukenuk threatened peace in the region.

With the treaty signed and sent off to Washington, Harrison returned to Vincennes to resume his duties as Indiana territorial governor. In Washington the Senate ratified the agreement on January 25, 1805, and then turned its attention to other matters. If officials at St. Louis thought that the agreement would end the relentless Indian raids, they soon realized the folly of such hopes. On July 1, 1805, General James Wilkinson, the new governor of Louisiana Territory, reached St. Louis. Soon after his arrival he met with a party of some 150 Sauks and Mesquakies who were waiting to see him. At the meeting Wilkinson sought to ease Indian discontent by giving the brother of the slain warrior the man's pardon from President Jefferson. The major point of the talks, however, focused on tribal discontent over the recent treaty. Tribal spokesmen admitted that although they had been "desirous to oblige the United States, . . . we had never before Sold Land, and we did not know the value of it . . . ." They went on to ask that Wilkinson find a way to give them something more than the meager compensation the treaty provided. Apparently the tribal spokesmen proved convincing because the governor recommended that the War Department consider a present to the tribes "to Secure the Confidence of these Nations." Nothing of the sort occurred.

While the Indians complained of having gotten too little for their lands, government officials strove to bring the long war between the Osages and the Sauks and Mesquakies to an end. In late summer, 1805, Governor Wilkinson sent messengers asking leaders from all three groups to come to St. Louis to attend a regional council. After weeks of waiting, during which intertribal raids continued unabated, representatives from nine tribes met on October 18 and signed a peace treaty. The agreement called for the Indians to settle their disputes peaceably, but if that became impossible they were to ask the American officials to settle the matter. The treaty signing did not bring much peace to the upper Mississippi River region, however, as gradual population pressures forced the tribes east of that stream to hunt ever farther beyond its western banks, encroaching on the lands of such tribes as the Sioux, Pawnee, and Osage and increasing the chances for violence and warfare.

Government officials at St. Louis feared that a combination of British and Spanish intrigue and the "jealousies of the Indians" would lead to renewed frontier violence as rumors of continuing Indian dissatisfaction reached them. As a result, the same week that governors Wilkinson and Harrison signed the peace treaty with the tribes of the Mississippi River region, they sent a delegation of Indian leaders to Washington. They assumed that once the chiefs had seen the size of the United States and its enormous population they would come to realize that war was out of the question. In fact, sending Indian delegations to the capital city became one of the preferred ways to try to persuade difficult tribes to remain at peace. On October 22, 1805, Wilkinson wrote that twenty-six persons from eleven tribes including the Sauks and Mesquakies, who comprised one-third of the group, would begin their journey east that same day. He went on to explain that the large number of Sauks and Mesquakies were included "in consideration of our very delicate standing with those Nations...."

Apparently not satisfied that the new treaty and the trip to Washington by themselves would ensure a stable peace, the two governors continued to fear the worst. In fact, the day after they signed the peace treaty and even before the tribal leaders began their trek east, the two men reported that they thought that "the Indians of the Mississippi...will embrace the earliest occasion to strike our frontiers...." To prevent this they advised the War Department to station troops at Prairie du Chien, where the Wisconsin River enters the Mississippi, directly in the heart of Sauk, Mesquakie, Winnebago, and Sioux country. Wilkinson had sent Lieutenant Zebulon M. Pike up the Mississippi in September that same year to locate potential sites for new military posts among the Indians, and Pike's travels that fall and winter confirmed the mouth of the Wisconsin as a strategic location for an army post.

While the territorial officials sent their dispatches expressing fear of continuing Indian violence, Stoddard led the tribal emissaries on their trip east. They rode government-provided horses to Louisville, where they boarded Ohio River keelboats to Wheeling. From there they went through the mountains by carriage and reached Washington in time to meet President Jefferson in early January. He promised the delegation that the government would establish trading posts in their country, piously telling them that the government wanted "no profit in that business" but rather wanted to satisfy their needs for manufactured goods. The president urged peace among the tribes and gave the United States as an example for the chiefs to follow. "We are numerous as the Stars in the Heavens and we are all gunmen," he noted. "Yet we live in peace and friendship with all Nations." Before Jefferson dismissed the tribal leaders, he invited them to visit Philadelphia, Baltimore, and New York to get a clear understanding of American strength.

Their tour of the East may well have impressed the few chiefs who made the trip, but their experiences and new understanding of the size of the United States had no immediate effect on the frontier situation. Sauk and Mesquakie war parties continued to leave the villages for attacks upon the hated Osages in present Missouri. Within only a few weeks of signing the intertribal accord in October 1805, violence flared anew, and on December 10 that year Wilkinson noted that the Sauks, Mesquakies, and Iowas "are certainly disposed for war," and blamed their continuing hostilities on British traders from Canada and French and Spanish merchants still in Illinois and Missouri. In the three weeks preceding this report, the governor had learned of new attacks on the frontier settlements. He thought that warriors from the Mississippi River villages, unable to find any Osage victims, had turned their wrath on pioneer whites nearby. That autumn Sauk and Mesquakie warriors killed two white hunters in one attack, while other war parties raided a salt works up the Missouri River and killed yet another man at another salt works in eastern Iowa.

Wilkinson hurried to settle the situation short of war when he received the reports of the continuing depredations. He called yet another council with Sauk village leaders, and when they arrived in St. Louis he sternly reminded them of their recent treaty agreement. Then he accused them of having broken that pact repeatedly and demanded that they surrender to him the warriors responsible for the recent attacks within the next several months. He assured the chiefs that the "big knives," as the Sauks called the Americans, wanted to remain at peace, but he assured them that the hostile actions of their young men would surely bring war. If they continued their raids, he threatened that the Great Father would "turn loose his Warriors" who were "as numerous as the trees in the woods," and who would destroy the tribe, as they had other Indians farther east. Of more immediate importance to his assembled listeners, Wilkinson vowed to cut off the Indian's trade so that they would not even be able to get a "blanket, a gun or a charge of Powder." The Sauks had been asking for improved trade relations for some years, and this threat struck at the heart of their fragile economy. Still, the governor's demands brought little respite from the attacks.

When the Sauk leaders failed to release their Osage prisoners and ignored Wilkinson's demand that they surrender those guilty of the autumn 1805 raids, the governor decided to send troops to Saukenuk. Perhaps, Wilkinson speculated, seeing soldiers in their village might bring some positive response, so early in 1806 he ordered a detachment north. Commanded by Captain James Many, the soldiers looked for potential sites for a new military installation, tried to gain the release of the Osage prisoners, and delivered yet another "strong talk" to the Sauk leaders. After landing his detachment north of the mouth of the Wisconsin River, the Captain decided to suggest Prairie du Chien as the best place for a new military post. Then, accompanied by some Winnebago and Menominee warriors, the troops started back down the Mississippi River. When he reached the Rock River, Many learned that the Sauk villagers had just finished a drinking bout and that they were in no mood to welcome visitors. Recklessly he stopped anyway.

Instead of extending the usual gracious welcome that Indians traditionally gave to visitors, drunken warriors, shouting and cursing the "bloody Americans" for having killed some of their relatives, confronted the officer and his men. Captain Many hastily retired across the river from the village, but some of the Sauks followed with their weapons concealed under their blankets. When the Captain asked about the Osage hostages, they abruptly changed the subject. Pointing to the pompon atop the officer's hat, they belligerently accused him of wearing a feather as a symbol of hostility toward them. As the warriors became more insulting and fighting seemed about to erupt, Lieutenant Pike arrived with reinforcements. Nevertheless, the two officers made little headway in calming the Sauks, and the villagers told the officers' Winnebago and Menominee companions that the whites planned to poison them if they accompanied them farther down the river. The Indians guiding the soldiers ignored the warnings, and when the hostility subsided even ransomed two of the Osage prisoners held at the village. Certain that some of the warriors had wanted to attack his troops, Captain Many headed back down the Mississippi to St. Louis.

Despite the failure of the 1805 treaty to bring peace between the Sauks and the United States during the first decade of the nineteenth century, tribal leaders had accepted the fact that war against the big knives remained out of the question. When they grudgingly accepted the 1804 treaty ceding all their lands east of the Mississippi without immediate warfare, the Sauks had signaled their unwillingness to fight. However much they objected to that agreement, because it had been negotiated with minor chiefs not delegated to surrender any tribal land, and no matter how much they complained about how little they had received in benefits, they accepted the treaty as valid. In the rapidly changing circumstances that swirled around them, the Sauk chiefs struggled to keep their people out of war, sometimes unsuccessfully, for the next decade.

In the face of continuing demands for war voiced by dissidents and insubordinate warriors, the patience and skills of the village leaders were tried repeatedly. Their efforts to maintain peace even led to the physical withdrawal of some agitated groups from the tribe. During the pre-1812 years, however, the peace chiefs retained nominal if shaky control as they faced an often rebellious and belligerent minority. American authorities in the region frequently reported rumors of conspiracies, threats of violence, and their fears of Indian attacks to Washington. For example, during the summer of 1806, Harrison wrote Jefferson that the Sauk and Kickapoo tribes were even then circulating wampum belts calling for war against the United States. Similar reports continued to surface until the War of 1812 ended any doubt the U.S. government had about tribal allegiances in the upper Mississippi Valley.

Even had all the Mississippi Valley tribes wished to live in peace as the nineteenth century proceeded, events elsewhere kept their situation unsettled. The Indian fear that the whites would soon take their land proved to be well-founded during the first decade of the century. Harrison not only stripped the Sauks and Mesquakies of most of their territory, but did the same to many other tribes of the region. With the 1802 Treaty of Vincennes, he and other territorial governors began extracting land from the Indians. By 1807 the United States had purchased or taken eastern Michigan, all but a small portion of northwestern Ohio, the southern third of Indiana, and most of Illinois. While the federal officials acquired the land, pioneers by the thousands rushed in to settle it, and the government established new territories and states quickly. Ohio became the first state north of the Ohio River and by 1812 had over 250,000 inhabitants. Indiana became a separate territory in 1800 and by 1812 some 25,000 settlers lived there. Illinois Territory began in 1809, and three years later it claimed at least 13,000 inhabitants.

The Sauks and Mesquakies living along the Mississippi River knew little of these events, but the pattern of rapid expansion that developed during the 1800–1812 era proved inescapable. The whites had come into Indian country, and as they came they took land from every tribe in their path. These events kept the situation in the upper Mississippi Valley and the Great Lakes region in a state of turmoil until after the War of 1812, and Indian resistance to the continuing white encroachments began in what is now Indiana and Michigan.

Groups of Sauks, Mesquakies, Kickapoos, Potawatomis, and other midwestern tribes regularly traveled to Drummond's Island in Lake Huron or Fort Malden at Amherstburg in Upper Canada. Just a few miles across the river from Detroit, Fort

Malden housed British Indian Office agents and traders. Through their annual meetings with tribes from the United States, the men at the fort gathered intelligence data on U.S.-Indian relations in the region south of the Great Lakes. They also gave presents and advice to their tribal visitors: the American frontier officials felt that the British were poisoning the Indians' minds against the United States. There is little doubt that Black Hawk and his Sauk companions enjoyed their trips to Canada and appreciated the hospitality and gifts provided by the King's agents there. In fact, they crossed Illinois, Indiana, and Michigan so regularly on their trips to Amherstburg that by 1820 their path became known as the Great Sauk Trail.

Meanwhile, events in the Midwest moved quickly toward the War of 1812. By 1807, American frontier officials noted increased restlessness and violence among the Indians. Reports from Chicago and the upper Mississippi detailed widespread talk of war, but no fighting occurred there. In 1808, regular army troops moved up the Mississippi to begin construction of Fort Madison, about fifteen miles north of the Des Moines River. When the Sauks learned of this they held several councils to discuss the move's implications. Black Hawk recalled that the soldiers "had brought great guns [artillery] with them—and look like a war party of whites" invading their country. The alarmed chiefs met Lieutenant Alpha Kingsley, who commanded the detachment, and he assured them that his men were building the quarters for a government trader who would sell the Indians the goods they needed.

The Sauks disbelieved the whites because they saw that there were more buildings than any trader could use, but the officers explained that the other structures would house soldiers who would keep the trader company. During the winter of 1808-09, construction slowed, but the next spring the soldiers went back to work on the fort. By then the Indians had decided that they could live without a trading post if having one meant bringing troops into their country. In early 1809, according to Black Hawk, Sauk warriors spied on the garrison, visited it, and hunted nearby. They harassed work details by attempting to steal their weapons and by sneaking up on and surprising troops when they strayed far from the construction site. Apparently these actions terrified Lieutenant Kingsley because he sent frantic requests for reinforcements, predicting the destruction of the entire garrison unless he got more men. His reading of the situation appears to have been correct.

Frequently Black Hawk and a large number of Sauk warriors visited the construction site, trading minor items with the soldiers and causing trouble. To avoid being surprised by a night attack on the still uncompleted fort, Kingsley ordered all of his men to sleep with their weapons and kept some of them tending large fires from 100 to 200 yards from the unfinished stockade. Hoping to defuse what he deemed a dangerous situation, Kingsley called the Sauk leaders into the fort for a council. This further excited the warriors, who rushed to the stockade walls for a better view. Standing on blocks of wood, old barrels, and whatever else they could find, the warriors peered into the fort. The mere presence of the Indians might not have frightened the garrison, but the fact that all of the onlookers held weapons certainly did. Later Black Hawk excused the Indians' action of standing around the walls of the fort armed with guns or with bows and arrows because "the soldiers had their guns loaded."

While the officers and chiefs talked, the warriors began to dance outside the fort. Moving toward the post gate, they pushed past the guards, hoping to gain entrance. As soon as the Indians began to crowd in, the officers ended their council with the chiefs brusquely and ordered the troops into formation. Soldiers spilled out of the buildings, their muskets at the ready, and the braves halted abruptly. Instead of being able to rush pell-mell into the fort, they faced ranks of armed soldiers and a loaded cannon, flanked by an artilleryman holding a lighted fuse. While the Indians wanted to attack and destroy the garrison none was so foolish as to rush into the face of certain death, so they left "the fort with a yell." Black Hawk recalled that the Sauks had not planned to attack in that manner, but he admitted that had the warriors gained entrance to the fort "all the whites would have been killed."

The growing strain between the United States and Great Britain and increased Indian-white tensions on the frontier aroused Black Hawk's anti-American feelings. Despite complaints from frontier officials that the frequent land cessions demanded by the government infuriated the tribes, policymakers in the East ignored or chose to disbelieve their western counterparts. By 1807 the Shawnee prophet Tenskwatawa (known simply as the Prophet) began to complicate matters. His new religious doctrines and strongly anti-American ideas had swept through the tribes in Indiana, Michigan, Wisconsin, and Illinois. While the Rock River Sauks remained on the fringes of the area most affected by the Prophet's dogma, in the summer of 1807, Main Poc, a Potawatomi healer and medicine man, visited them with the Prophet's message. He urged the Sauks, Mesquakies, and Winnebagoes to accept Tenskwatawa's teachings, and encouraged them to move east to the Prophet's settlement on the Wabash River in Indiana. Main Poc warned that if the western villagers refused to join their eastern friends that the Americans would eventually take Saukenuk. At the time few Sauks responded to Main Poc. In fact, Black Hawk noted that he assumed the visiting shaman "used these arguments merely to encourage us to join him," but "we agreed that we would not."

Although the Sauks and Mesquakies failed to heed the Prophet's call, their unrest and dissatisfaction with the United States continued. Ironically, while American frontier officials complained that the British exerted undue influence over their tribal charges, British officials feared the opposite. Despite annual visits from many tribes within the United States, officials at Amherstburg were delighted in 1808 when the Prophet sent news that he planned to visit them in Canada. Although Tenskwatawa chose to send his brother Tecumseh in his place, the British hoped that the visit was a signal that their influence was increasing. Nevertheless, the British authorities in Canada continued to fear the Indians as potential enemies. The Gover-

nor General at Montreal recommended that the Crown enlarge
the Indian Department. If not, he wrote, British inaction would
force the tribes to ally themselves with the American government. Although they might "be of little use as friends," he cau-
tioned that it was essential "to prevent them from becoming
enemies."

As various contingents of Indians dealt alternately with the
British and the Americans, the situation remained chaotic. The
United States government continued to press compliant chiefs
to sell ever more land while advocating the settlement of increasing numbers of pioneers in the areas near the tribes. This policy
forced the Indians into an ever-decreasing land area, making
their lives more difficult each year. Angry Sauk and Mesquakie
warriors complained repeatedly about the tide of pioneer settlement, but that only attracted the attention of American officials
responsible for achieving peace. By the summer of 1808, Sauk
warriors traveling though Indiana to visit the Prophet vowed
that it was "the intention of their tribe to support the prophet
against all his enemies." A year later William Clark, who since
his return from the famed exploratory expedition had become
the Indian agent for the tribes in the Louisiana Territory, reported from St. Louis that the Prophet's messengers had tried to
persuade the Sauks, Kickapoos, and other tribes living in Illinois to go to war against the pioneer settlers.

According to frontier officials, by the summer of 1810, large
numbers of Sauks and Mesquakies appeared ready to join the
Prophet in Indiana. On June 15, Governor Harrison reported
news that some 1,100 Sauks, Mesquakies, and Winnebagoes, as
well as one of the Potawatomi villages, had decided to move to
Prophetstown. While that relocation would have included entire
families rather than just warriors, further rumors suggested that
the Sauks had prepared themselves to fight. And while some of
the Indians may actually have considered war against the Americans, no conflict occurred. Instead, even the most belligerent
warriors usually left the settlers alone and continued to travel to
Canada to get presents and kind words from their British father.
As they returned to the Prophet's settlement and west to their Il-

linois villages, the disgruntled Indians sought other tribes as allies, but rarely for anti-American activities.

Rather than attack the pioneers, most Indians pursued their traditional enemies. For example, that same year, 1810, Sauk, Mesquakie, Kickapoo, and Winnebago war parties left their villages in central and western Illinois and southern Wisconsin, crossed the Mississippi, and raided the Osages. Undoubtedly Black Hawk participated in some of these raids. When the allied tribesmen failed to locate their quarry, they stole livestock from and occasionally killed pioneers, but they apparently did not threaten any large-scale violence. That changed abruptly in 1811 when American miners tried to take the Dubuque mines from the Mesquakies. Located on the west side of the Mississippi, the mines had provided the Mesquakies a readily available supply of lead for musketballs. Even more important, it gave them a valuable commodity to sell to the traders. In the late 1780s, Mesquakie chiefs had leased some of the lead lands to Julian Dubuque, but they agreed that the lease ran only until his death or until he abandoned the area.

Despite his agreement with the Indians, Dubuque had gotten a title to the lead region from the Spanish government, and when he died his heirs sold his presumed landrights to some Americans. They hired about sixty men and early in 1811 set off up the Mississippi to begin large-scale work at the mines. The Mesquakies and Sauks objected heatedly, refusing to let the Americans even beach their boats and threatening to kill them all. Nicholas Boilvin, the Indian agent at Prairie du Chien, persuaded the outraged Indians to let the heirs sell Dubuque's equipment at the mines, and convinced the would-be miners that they had to leave. As soon as the whites left, the warriors burnt all of the buildings to the ground, swearing "never to give up their land until they all were dead."

By late that same spring, word reached St. Louis that the Prophet had sent war belts to the Mississippi Valley tribes and that some of the Sauks had decided to go to war. While the whites worried about the truth of the rumors, the Sauks visited the British to get supplies because poor hunting had created a desperate need for food and clothing. By the end of the summer of 1811, at least three hundred Sauks met the British Indian agent, Matthew Elliot, at Fort Malden. He gave each warrior a rifle or musket, plenty of powder and lead, as well as blankets, cloth, shirts, and smaller items. Although generous, the gifts came with a warning from Elliot—stay at peace with the Americans. He told them they would surely lose any such conflict, and after feeding the group he sent them back to their homes in Illinois.

Nevertheless, the threat of a frontier Indian conflict would not die because the Indians had legitimate grievances that the government refused to consider. On their way home from Malden, the Sauks and Mesquakies stopped at Prophetstown to visit Tecumseh and the Prophet. Despite their obvious interest in the movement that the Shawnee brothers led, the Rock River Indians remained divided over how to respond. Tenskwatawa's teachings failed to capture their imaginations, and Tecumseh's call for a multitribal confederation to block continuing white expansion did not persuasde them either. Apparently the Sauks lived just far enough from the activities in Indiana to avoid becoming tied closely to the Shawnee brothers' cause. When the Illinois Indians reached Prophetstown, they learned that Tecumseh had begun a long journey through the South to attract some of the major tribes there to his confederacy. Although the Shawnee leader spent nearly six months on this trip, his recruiting efforts largely failed.

In fact, his absence from Prophetstown set into motion events that destroyed his hopes to block American expansion and led at least indirectly to many tribes going to war. When Governor Harrison learned of Tecumseh's absence he reported that the British had sent large amounts of supplies to Prophetstown, and he sought permission to destroy the Indian confederacy centered there. By August 1811, Harrison received orders that allowed him to move cautiously but to attack if he thought that the Indians there posed a threat to peace. Wasting little time, Harrison gathered his forces and marched north to attack Prophetstown in November. At the Battle of Tippecanoe he defeated the warriors under Tenskwatawa. This offensive drove many of the northern tribes into the arms of the British, and when large-scale fighting between the United States and Great Britain began in 1812, the tribesmen viewed the British as their only hope for retaining their homeland.

Actually, American ineptitude and greed coupled with Indian resentment triggered much of the trouble. Many Indians had made the trek to Fort Malden to visit the British in order to get much-needed food, blankets, guns, and ammunition because, they claimed, these goods were unavailable from their usual traders. Poor weather had hurt Indian crops during the summer of 1811 and with the trade breakdown that autumn they had become desperate. At Prairie du Chien, Agent Boilvin did what he could, feeding several thousand of the nearly destitute Indians for up to a month. He met with leaders from Sioux, Winnebago, Sauk, and Mesquakie bands trying to persuade them to remain peaceful. In their discussions with him, the Indians admitted that British agents moved freely through the country and that they had asked the tribes to join the British when the war began. Because the federal government had decided to encourage the tribes to remain neutral and at peace, there was little that the agent could tell his charges to counter the British enticements.

Clark persuaded chiefs of several nearby tribes, including the Sauks and Mesquakies, to accompany him to Washington. They set out in June, just as Congress prepared to declare war against Britain, and did not return until that November. Obviously, with some of the peace chiefs no longer present, those favoring war gained more immediate influence within the tribes. When news of the U.S. declaration of war against Great Britain reached the upper Mississippi Valley, warriors from the tribes of the region met in council at Saukenuk. Several frontier newspapers reported that the Winnebagoes, Kickapoos, Potawatomis, Shawnees, and Miamis had voted for war against the U.S. Despite the presence of the Prophet's representatives at the meeting, others, including some of the Sauks and Mesquakies, held back. While the remaining leaders of these tribes opposed war, others prepared to fight.

In fact, even as the grand council broke up, warriors from many tribes, including the Sauks and Mesquakies, gathered near Peoria (Illinois) and declared that "they would attack the Americans in the dark of the moon." As usual, village civil chiefs tried to dissuade the young men from doing anything that they thought would endanger the tribe, but their control of the situation weakened steadily. They could advise the warriors not to join the newly forming war parties, and might even try to get the village women to dissuade their husbands and sons. However, the chiefs had no means to demand or coerce obedience, and the warriors did as they pleased. While the discussions continued, Black Hawk visited the Peoria Lake villages. He claimed that he wanted to talk with a Thomas Forsyth, a trader who resided there, but probably met with Main Poc instead.

At that point Black Hawk remained uncertain about what to do, and his confusion probably reflected the thinking of many Indians of that region. He reported that the British agent, Colonel Robert Dickson, traveled from one village to another holding councils, making promises, and giving presents to his listeners. Yet at this point the Sauk warrior had not decided whether to join the British and attack the western American settlements or to remain neutral. Recalling his indecision years later, Black Hawk said that "he had not discovered one good trait in the character of the Americans that had come to the country! They made fair promises but never fulfilled them!" Admitting his confusion over white attitudes and actions, he remarked that "their feelings are acted upon by certain rules laid down by their preachers! whilst ours are governed only by the monitor within us." Black Hawk wanted to know why the spirits had sent the whites "to drive us from our homes, and introduce among us poisonous liquors, disease, and death?" Despite such views, he remained at peace for several months.

Black Hawk never clearly articulated the reasons why he and many of the other Sauks went to war against the United States in 1812, but the events of that year that led up to the decision are easy to trace. Surely his distrust of the Americans and anger at their having begun moving into Sauk territory helped persuade him to oppose the advancing "Big Knives." Relative isolation and lack of information about the whites perhaps played a role too. Had the war leader known anything about the size of the United States or the determination of both its government and its people to crush the Indians, he might well have moved west ahead of the pioneers then flooding into the Mississippi Valley. In the summer of 1812, however, Black Hawk knew little of these things, so it was not surprising that when a force of some two hundred Winnebago warriors passed Saukenuk on its way to attack the troops at Fort Madison, he joined, leading a contingent of Sauks.

On September 5, the Indians attacked the post during the late afternoon, but they had no way to breach its sturdy log walls. Having failed in their assault, the Indians remained hidden the next day. Their spies had learned that each morning the troops marched out to drill or to perform work details, so when the drums inside the fort began to beat, the warriors expected the soldiers to fall into their hands. Instead a lone man came out and walked down to the river. After he returned without incident, four more men went down to gather wood. While they worked at the riverbank, another soldier walked from the post. This proved too much for the impatient warriors, and they shot and scalped him. The woodcutters fled toward the gate, but shots from Indian guns killed two of them. Now the firing began in earnest as both sides shot at anything that moved. Several times the Indians set fire to buildings inside the stockade, but the soldiers extinguished the blazes before they caused major damage. On September 9, after several days of sporadic shooting, the Indians realized that their siege had failed. They had little to shoot at as the log stockade protected the fifty or so men inside. So when their ammunition ran low, they broke off the assault, having lost a single warrior and without killing any more whites than the three who died outside the fort on the first morning.

Other attacks soon followed. Some four hundred warriors raided the scattered pioneers then living in eastern Missouri near Portage des Sioux, wounding several people and stealing horses and cattle. Units of frontier rangers (mounted militiamen) tried to defend the settlers but often could do little more than respond to reports of attacks rather than prevent them. In the case of the September 1812 incidents, the volunteers overtook the raiders but had too few men to dare fight such a large Indian force. Although the rangers destroyed a few of the Indian canoes, the warriors escaped with their spoils using their remaining seventy canoes. In October 1812, Illinois governor Ninian Edwards ordered the rangers north to the Peoria area, where they destroyed three villages and forced the inhabitants to flee. Many of the refugees sought help at Saukenuk, so the Rock River villagers saw first-hand what might happen if the whites struck back successfully.

Continuing American mismanagement or willful misunderstanding did nothing to help matters in the Illinois country. When the Sauk chiefs who had accompanied William Clark to Washington returned in early November 1812, they reported that the Great Father had asked the tribes to remain neutral. He had told them that the United States wanted the Indians to "hunt and support our families. . . ." The chiefs understood President Madison to have promised them that the American factor (government fur trader) at Fort Madison would supply them "on credit, as the British traders had done." However, this was a falsehood because by law the factor could not give the Indians any goods on credit. Nevertheless, the delegation's account of their trip east and how well the whites had received them pleased most of the villagers. Even Black Hawk seemed impressed by the chiefs' good reports and talked about staying neutral.

When the time came for the Sauks to disperse to their winter hunting grounds, they traveled to Fort Madison where the situation changed abruptly. At a short council, the local commander gave them some pipes, tobacco, and a little food as presents.

Then the trader strode in, and the Indians greeted him warmly, as they depended on his goods to get their people through the winter hunting season. To the visitors' dismay the trader said nothing about provisions for the coming months, so Black Hawk explained that the Sauks had decided to accept the president's advice and remain at peace. When he asked for the eagerly anticipated food and supplies, the trader's reply shocked the assemblage. The trader assured them that he had plenty of the things they wanted, but insisted that they would have to pay for them. He had no orders to extend credit to the Indians. To men so dependent upon credit for their food, clothing, guns, and ammunition, the news was devastating. Confused and angry, the chiefs protested that the president had assured them that they could get credit—but both the post commander and the government trader said that they had no orders to change the usual cash policy.

"We left the fort dissatisfied, and went to our camp," Black Hawk said. There the discussions continued into the night as the desperate Indians tried to understand their new situation. Those who had been to Washington insisted that the president had promised them credit if they stayed out of the war. After an almost sleepless night of "gloom and discontent," the situation changed. Edward La Gouthrie, a long-time (British) trader with the Sauks, stopped at nearby Rock Island. News of his arrival with two boatloads of presents swept through the Indian camp. Hurriedly taking down their lodges, the Sauks moved to the trader's camp while singing, beating their drums, and firing muskets into the air. La Gouthrie welcomed them warmly and sat down to smoke. Then, standing near his British flag, he told them that agent Dickson had sent presents to them, including a large British flag, a keg of rum, and smaller items.

The next morning the trader met with the Sauks again. This time they asked for the goods on his two boats and promised to pay for them with furs the next spring. La Gouthrie agreed to this promptly, and while the Indians divided the trader's items, he took Black Hawk aside and asked for his help. He told the warrior that Dickson was at Green Bay with plenty of supplies, guns, and ammunition, and that he sought Indian allies. La Gouthrie urged the Sauk warrior to organize a war party and travel to Green Bay as quickly as possible. Black Hawk agreed and hurriedly gathered some two hundred men for the journey. As he explained the events later, the trader's fortuitous arrival at Rock Island had tipped the scales from peace to war. Staying neutral and cooperating with the Americans had brought the Sauks face-to-face with potential starvation. Without credit they could not survive the winter. The British, however, provided presents, essential supplies on credit, and a chance for the warriors, to get back into action. For Black Hawk that ended any hopes that the Sauks might avoid the conflict. As he depicted the situation, the Indians had "been forced into war by being deceived" by the Americans.

The reasons for the Sauks' entry into the war as British allies proved more complicated than Black Hawk's account suggested. In fact, most of the tribe still preferred neutrality, and even those who opted for war may have felt that there was little choice. Certainly the lack of trade goods from the Americans proved crucial, but many of their neighbors and allies sided with the British. Even if the Sauks stayed out of the white men's war, hostility from the neighboring tribes such as the Kickapoos, Potawatomis, Sioux, and Winnebagoes in particular would have brought violence and destruction into their country. The Sauk warrior ignored all of these reasons for joining the British, but they existed in 1812 and certainly he must have been at least dimly aware of them.

At Green Bay the Sauk force joined with contingents of Ottawa, Kickapoo, Winnebago, and Potawatomi warriors already there. Colonel Dickson had provided plenty of guns, ammunition, food, and drink for the warriors, and Black Hawk reported that they were in "high spirits." That same evening, Dickson sent for the Sauk leader and addressed him as General Black Hawk. More significantly, he explained what the British hoped to do and asked that the Sauks become British allies. Telling the war leader that the English knew that the Americans wanted to seize tribal lands, he assured his attentive listener that the King had sent Dickson and troops to drive the Americans back to their own country. Whatever else Dickson may have said, Black Hawk remembered the talk as a pledge of mutual support and a promise to defend his tribal homeland. The warrior had no love for the Americans, and Dickson's words appealed to his pride, his sense of identity as a Sauk, and his proprietary feelings toward Saukenuk. He saw no reason to reject Dickson's offer and stayed on the British side throughout the rest of the war.

Black Hawk proposed launching a series of raids down the Mississippi River, but Dickson convinced him that he could do more damage to the Americans elsewhere. Playing on his listener's sense of honor, the agent explained that there would be soldiers rather than just women and children to fight at Detroit. He promised that if the Indians defeated the American forces there, they could return to attack the Americans in the Mississippi country later. That pleased the Sauk. During the meeting the British agent gave Black Hawk a large medal, a paper commission, and a British flag. What a warrior was to do with such items hundreds of miles from his lodge is uncertain, but they provided a powerful symbol of the alliance with the King. After providing them new weapons, ammunition, and clothing, Dickson treated the warriors to an evening-long dance and feast.

Early the next morning, Black Hawk, Dickson, and about five hundred warriors set out for Detroit via present Chicago. They passed the abandoned Fort Dearborn en route and rode on across Michigan. In January 1813 the combined forces of English and Indians attacked an American force under James Winchester in what became known as the Battle of Frenchtown. After initially being repulsed, Colonel Henry Proctor's troops forced the Americans to surrender. Black Hawk reported with some surprise that "the Americans fought well, and drove us with considerable loss!" He had been under the impression that they could not fight effectively. After this battle the campaign ended for the winter and Black Hawk stayed with the British forces near Detroit. Later in the spring he took part in the attack on Fort Meigs on the Maumee River.

For that campaign General Proctor moved a strong force of British regulars and Canadian militiamen south across southeastern Michigan. By May 1, 1813, his combined Indian and-British force had reached its destination. Some 1,200 Indians under the command of Tecumseh surrounded the post to prevent anyone from leaving or entering it. Black Hawk and the other warriors waited impatiently while the British artillery blasted futilely at the well-entrenched fort. Then American reinforcements arrived by boat, but instead of entering the fort they launched a surprise attack on the British artillery positions. Driving Proctor's men back, they advanced too far, and the reformed British and Indian units surrounded and captured all but some 150 of the 800 attackers. Flushed with victory, the warriors made their captives run the gauntlet, killing nearly forty of them before Indian leaders reasserted control and halted the slaughter.

The British had promised the Indians who became their allies that they had fought to enforce the 1795 Greenville Treaty line as the border separating the tribes from the Americans. Because reestablishing that line would have restored virtually all of Illinois and Indiana to the tribes, the British promises provided a strong inducement to fight. Still the warriors had little patience for besieging a well-fortified position, and only a week after the victory at Fort Meigs the Sauks and others left. With his allies gone and many of the Canadian militiamen anxious to return home to plant their crops, Proctor lifted the siege on May 9 and returned to Canada.

As spring faded into summer, several thousand Indians gathered at Detroit. Many warriors had brought their dependents there for the British to protect and feed while they fought alongside the regular troops. Although his commissary officers complained bitterly about the Indians' depleting the food supplies, the warriors convinced Proctor to launch another assault on Fort Meigs. Unfortunately for the attackers, they lacked trans-

portation for heavy artillery, and the defenders had strengthened
their position since the siege in early May. Nevertheless, the British
and Indian force reached the fort on July 21, 1813, and attacked.
Proctor's light artillery pieces had little effect on the sturdy fort. As
a result, Black Hawk and his companions stayed in the woods, although at one point some of the warriors staged a mock battle, apparently hoping to persuade the defenders that a relief column
headed for the fort needed their help. This ruse, like the British artillery, failed, so after a week Proctor withdrew.

Four days later, on August 2, Proctor's force attacked Fort
Stephenson, about thirty-five miles farther east. There the British felt confident of capturing the small garrison, even calling
for its surrender before launching their attack. The Americans
rejected the British demands, however, and defended themselves
stoutly. When the light artillery again failed to breach the stockade, Proctor ordered an attack. The regulars marched against
the front wall of the fort while the Indians flanked one of the
sides. Waiting until their enemies came to within point-blank
range, the defenders fired a devastating volley into the massed
troops. Although Black Hawk praised the British regulars' bravery, he reported that they "were defeated, and a great number
killed." As Proctor prepared to retreat, some of the discouraged
Indians began leaving for their homes, while others returned to
Detroit.

There is some confusion about when Black Hawk and his
Sauk companions left the British forces to head back to Illinois.
Just a year or two before his death, he told an Iowa neighbor
that he had fought in the October 5, 1813, Battle of the Thames
and that he had seen Tecumseh killed by the attacking Americans. Although he failed to mention this in his autobiography,
he knew the details of the battle well, even identifying two Potawatomi leaders, Billy Caldwell and Shabbona, as participants at
the Thames. At the time, few whites or Indians knew which
chiefs had been present, although it seems likely that someone
on the Iowa frontier might have put such the names into the aging Sauk's mouth.

In any event, sometime in late 1813 the Sauk left the retreating British army to head home. "I was now tired of being with them—our success being bad, and having got no plunder," Black Hawk recalled. "That night I took about twenty of my braves and left the British camp for home." To a traditional warrior there was no shame in leaving during the middle of a campaign, particularly one in which the leaders exhibited a lack of good sense. In addition, having been away from Saukenuk for months, the men had felt some responsibility to go home to help feed their families.

The Saukenuk villagers welcomed the warriors back with the usual feasting and story-telling sessions, but Black Hawk and his men had little positive to report as they ridiculed British tactics and their apparent lack of good judgment. In fact, while the Sauk leader praised their bravery, he denounced the whites in both armies. "Instead of stealing upon each other, and taking every advantage to kill the enemy and save their own people," he reported, "they march out into the open daylight, and fight, regardless of the number of warriors they may lose!" Then, he continued, after the battle they neither celebrate their achievement nor mourn their losses. Instead the leaders on each side write reports, always claiming a victory for their troops and reporting less than half the numbers of casualties they suffered. The British gave their troops better clothing and food, but Black Hawk thought that the Americans fired more accurately during the fighting. Overall, he claimed that the whites' officers were unfit to lead troops into battle, and he expressed contempt for the whites as warriors.

While Black Hawk and several hundred of the warriors had campaigned alongside the British in Ohio and Michigan, Illinois governor Ninian Edwards and Missouri governor William Clark had persuaded the neutral Sauks and Mesquakies to move away from their pro-British relatives. By mid-1813 the villages of supposedly friendly Sauks, Mesquakies, Iowas, and Kickapoos had relocated to the area at the mouth of the Des Moines River in Iowa. That still left the neutrals too close to the hostile bands, so frontier officials continued their efforts to separate the hostile from the peaceful Indians. After several councils at St. Louis during mid-1813, in September of that year Clark met the friendly villagers at Portage des Sioux. There he persuaded them that they could live more safely if they shifted their villages once more—this time to Osage lands along the Missouri, near the mouth of the Grand River. He promised that their factor John Johnson would move the government trading post there so that they would not lack supplies, and on September 28 the Indian leaders agreed.

By the end of the year nearly 1,500 of the villagers had migrated to this new location. Their midwar migration resulted from the continuing ambivalence the Sauks and their neighbors felt about the conflict. When directly threatened or promised gifts and protection by the Americans, they tended to remain at peace. Otherwise they raided occasionally. It also demonstrates the continuing rifts between the advocates of peace and war within individual villages and the tribes as a whole. With those favoring war absent much of the time, the peace chiefs continued to exercise broad authority, and that certainly weakened the influence of Black Hawk and other war-minded leaders within the Sauk and Mesquakie tribes.

Another incident during the autumn of 1813 changed Black Hawk's position within his home village permanently. Up to that time he remained a highly respected war leader, although not a chief. While he and the other warriors remained in the East as British allies, the Missouri and Illinois militias campaigned steadily against the Indians in those areas. During September and October 1813, those troops pursued fleeing raiding parties, stormed villages suspected of harboring hostile warriors, and made life miserable for those Indians still in central and western Illinois. That autumn, while searching for hostile warriors along the Illinois River as far upstream as the Lake Peoria region, General Benjamin Howard sent Major Nathan Boone west toward the Rock River, but finding the villages along their route deserted, Boone's group stopped short of its destination and returned to Peoria.

At Saukenuk, the village scouts reported that the Americans were headed toward the village to attack. With many of the bravest warriors absent, the chiefs hesitated. After considerable debate they decided not to fight but to flee across the Mississippi temporarily. As one of the council members came out of the lodge, young Keokuk, the Watchful Fox, heard him talking about abandoning the village and asked to speak. Although he was not yet a recognized warrior, the chiefs invited him into the council lodge. There Keokuk gave a fiery speech denouncing his listeners as cowards for deciding to run rather than to fight. When he volunteered to lead the defense, the council placed him in command. Keokuk organized the warriors quickly and led one group of them toward the reportedly advancing Americans. The threat never materialized because the rangers had already started on their way back to Peoria, but Keokuk's actions so impressed the Saukenuk leaders that they chose him as the village war chief. That decision brought an immediate change to Black Hawk's life and role within the Sauk tribe. Prior to that event, the older man often spoke for the warriors when village decisions came up for discussion. Now the younger Keokuk, an excellent public speaker—Black Hawk was not—held a formally recognized position that outranked the older warrior's (within the village and the tribe as a whole). Soon the two men viewed each other as competitors, if not actual enemies, and their personal conflict helped pull the village society apart, as they rarely agreed or cooperated on important issues.

When Black Hawk and the other warriors returned to their village, they found major changes. The news that Keokuk had become war chief certainly jarred the older warrior, but that was not the only alteration he found. Equally important, he learned that perhaps as many as one-third of the Sauk and Mesquakie people had migrated to Missouri, where they became known as the Sauks and Mesquakies of the Missouri. (There they lived

under an uneasy truce with the Osage tribe and under the resentful gaze of the Missouri pioneers.) Not only that, but the
Sauk and Mesquakie in both Missouri and Illinois recognized
that the whites successful use of mounted rangers to raid Indian
villages and burn crops posed serious danger in the future. During the sugar-making season in early 1814, Black Hawk learned
of further American victories and that several of the other Illinois tribes had made peace.

In the summer of 1814, the Indians, British, and Americans all
resumed the fighting at one time or another. On May 1, Governor Clark led a two-hundred-man detachment up the Mississippi to build a fort at Prairie du Chien. From there Clark
assumed that American forces could prevent the British from
further supplying the restless tribes of that region and keep further raids into Missouri at a minimum. On his way north, Clark
stopped at the mouth of the Rock River where his forces hoped
to frighten the villagers into asking for peace. He demanded
that they move north and attack the Winnebagoes, still the most
anti-American people along the Mississippi, and the Sauks inti-
mated that they would do this. Then the Americans boarded
their five boats and continued up the river. They took Prairie du
Chien without firing a shot and began building what became
Fort Shelby. Clark returned to St. Louis to the cheers of the local
citizens for pacifying the region.

The optimism proved short-lived, however, because Indian
depredations continued in Missouri that spring and summer.
About the same time that Clark was leading his flotilla north,
reports of new Sauk and Mesquakie raids reached St. Louis.
Also, several Indians from the Rock River villages visited their
relatives in Missouri and ridiculed them for remaining at peace
with the Americans. By May 14, 1814, Sauk factor Johnson (in
Missouri) reported that as soon as the warriors from Saukenuk
had left, the Missouri Sauks began flying a British flag and became belligerent toward Americans. Because of this nearly open
hostility, Johnson and the Osage factor George Sibley abandoned their establishments and took the trade goods back to St.

Louis. Their caution proved wise because Indian forays continued throughout much of Missouri that spring, with isolated Indian attacks killing or wounding a number of pioneers and
terrorizing many others. Black Hawk's role in these hostilities
remains unclear, but he certainly supported the anti-American
actions. As the raiding increased and anti-Indian anger flared
across Missouri, many of the neutral Sauks and Mesquakies
who had moved there only a year earlier now fled back into Illinois and Iowa to escape retaliation.

Even while the tales of new depredations trickled into St.
Louis, Colonel William McKay, with another British force, re-
captured Prairie du Chien from the small garrison of American
regulars who had been left to defend the still-unfinished Fort
Shelby. Fearing that something of that sort might happen if they
did not get reinforcements up the Mississippi, Missouri officials
had just dispatched another unit to fortify Fort Shelby. The new
troops, commanded by Major John Campbell, set out up the
river in three keelboats with two supply barges. They stopped at
Rock River on July 14 to meet with the chiefs there. Campbell
reminded the Sauks of their earlier promise to raid the Winnebagoes, but they refused unless he would provide the necessary
arms and ammunition. After foolishly treating the Indians to
some whiskey, the whites adjourned the meeting and went into
camp nearby.

That night the situation changed dramatically. British agents
from Prairie du Chien arrived at Saukenuk bringing six kegs of
gunpowder and news of Colonel McKay's capture of the American fort. The traders called on the Sauks to rejoin the British
and attack the boats carrying the troops anchored nearby. Eager
to fight the Americans, Black Hawk gathered a force of warriors, and they moved quickly upriver to overtake Major Campbell's small flotilla. As the warriors caught up to the boats, a
strong headwind slowed the vessels, and soon Campbell's boat
ran aground. The major decided to halt there until the wind
slackened and sent most of his troops ashore to prepare break-
fast. When Black Hawk realized that Campbell had divided his

party the Sauk launched his attack. In the first volley the Indians killed or wounded all of the sentries, and by the time Campbell got his other men back on board, the Sauks had shot nearly half of them. As the warriors fired at the boat, Black Hawk shot flaming arrows into the sail lying on the deck, and soon it burst into flames.

When the officers on the other two boats realized that Campbell's vessel was afire, they turned back downstream to help. One of the two boats lost its anchor and drifted away helplessly, while the other drew alongside the burning craft to rescue the survivors. After throwing most of the provisions overboard to lighten their boat, the rangers hurriedly gathered the wounded and other survivors. Then they headed back downriver. The crew of the third vessel managed to get back into the current and escape as well.

As the Americans fled, Black Hawk and his men boarded the burning boat, put out the flames, and began salvaging what they could from the militia supplies still on board. They took several guns, large barrels of clothing, and even army tents back to Saukenuk. Having lost only three people while killing fourteen whites and wounding seventeen more, the Sauks and their allies danced and celebrated far into the night. So many of the dancers sported militia uniforms that evening that Black Hawk described the village as having "the appearance of a regular camp of soldiers." The victorious warriors danced around the scalp pole and showed their anti-American sentiments clearly. They flew the British flag at the center of Saukenuk, and showed off their spoils throughout the warm July night. At that point the Americans represented the party responsible for the loss of their land and the disruption of trade and hunting. The British, however, appeared to be strong friends willing to help the tribes push back the hated pioneers.

Only a few days after Black Hawk and the other villagers stopped celebrating, the British at Prairie du Chien learned of the Indians' victory. They responded immediately. Colonel McKay sent the Sauks ten kegs of gunpowder and other presents. The ammunition would help the Indians in their next battle against American troops when renewed fighting broke out a few weeks later. As soon as authorities in St. Louis heard of Major Campbell's disaster, they gathered another force of more than four hundred regulars and militiamen. Giving command to Major Zachary Taylor, General Howard sent the men upriver in eight boats. Taylor's instructions ordered him to destroy the Rock River villages and then to return downstream and build a new fort at the mouth of the Des Moines River.

By early September the American troops halted about a single day's travel from their goal. The next evening, September 4, Major Taylor's flotilla passed the mouth of the Rock and continued up the Mississippi as though headed for Prairie du Chien. While the Americans did that, British traders moving south slipped past them and delivered several artillery pieces from Fort Shelby to the Sauks. That night Black Hawk and his men helped the trader Duncan Graham dig the guns into position. While the Indians prepared for renewed combat, Taylor hoped to use a white flag to lure the Sauks into a council and then kill them. He never had a chance to do this because the Indians struck first. As the early sun started to burn off the mist on the river bottom land, the Sauks and British attacked. Their artillery poured an accurate fire into Taylor's boats, while other warriors raked his camp with musket fire. The Americans' small arms and artillery kept the Sauks at a distance temporarily, but when he realized that his troops could not survive the continuous attack by nearly 1,000 warriors, Taylor wisely ordered his men aboard the boats and fled back downstream. While the Sauks danced their victory celebration one more time, the major turned to building the new fort at the Des Moines River.

Black Hawk had hoped for a more extended battle because his men "had not yet had a fair fight with the Americans," but that was not to be. When Taylor decided that anything short of flight would bring disaster to his entire force, the Indians had to be content to follow the retreating Americans downstream and keep their activities under close surveillance. Fort Johnson, as the Americans called their new structure, stood on the east bank of the Mississippi, directly across from the mouth of the Des Moines River. Located on a small bluff about ninety feet high, it looked down upon the Des Moines rapids in the Mississippi as well. While the major reported on his location of the fort, the Sauks, Mesquakies, and other warriors remained nearby, hoping to ambush the building parties or to kill individual soldiers. Few chances occurred, and after a couple of isolated raids the warriors drifted back to their Rock River villages. Despite this, the soldiers abandoned the new fort by the end of October 1814 and again retreated to St. Louis.

The Indian victories over the Americans in the two battles near the Rock River brought the Sauks and Mesquakies continued British praise and a shower of presents. War parties left Prairie du Chien, newly supplied by British officers there, and raided south along the Mississippi River and into Missouri briefly during the autumn of 1814. That winter the Sauks and Mesquakies ignored the war and traveled west for their annual hunt, but by April 1815, Captain A. N. Bulger, the British commander at Prairie du Chien, urged the Indians to begin new raids on the settlements, and he continued to supply them with arms and ammunition. Gathering some 1,200 warriors from a half dozen tribes, Bulger promised the tribesmen that the British would help them retake the lands they had lost to the pioneers since the 1795 Treaty of Greenville. The captain claimed that a large number of British reinforcements would soon arrive at Quebec, and with that encouraging news he sent his eager listeners on a series of raids into Missouri. Throughout the spring and even into the summer of 1815, Sauk and Mesquakie warriors destroyed isolated farms, killed white individuals they encountered, stole horses and cattle, and generally wreaked havoc across the frontier.

While the attacks continued, news of the signing of the Treaty of Ghent slowly filtered out to the frontier. In the spring of 1815, the gunboat *Governor Clarke* stopped at the Rock River villages with news of the peace agreement, and the trader Duncan Graham hurried to Prairie du Chien with the news. When he learned that the war had ended, Captain Bulger worked desperately to recall the war parties he had so recently sent south, but his messengers failed to overtake several large ones. On May 10, 1815, the apologetic captain told a council of some eight hundred warriors that the conflict had ended. News that their allies had deserted them angered the Indians and even the usually reticent Black Hawk spoke bitterly. Waving the wampum he had received from the British nearly two years earlier, he shouted, "I have fought the Big Knives, and will continue to fight them till they are off our lands. Till then my father, your Red Children cannot be happy." Having had his say, he left the meeting quickly, organized another war party, and set off down the Mississippi.

Leaving Prairie du Chien, Black Hawk led the war party to the area between the Quivre River and Cap au Gris on the west bank of the Mississippi. There his force attacked several parties of whites, wounding, killing, and scalping as they went. Having descended the river in canoes, the warriors soon found themselves being pursued by mounted frontier rangers and had to fight for their lives. On May 24, a detachment of mounted troops from nearby Fort Howard overtook the war party, and Black Hawk foolishly led his men into a large sinkhole for shelter. At the bottom they hid behind a screen of bushes and dug small pits for protection. Aware that this position was precarious at best, some of the warriors began singing their death songs while the whites pushed a sort of cart up to the edge of the sinkhole for protection as they fired down on the Indians. After inconclusive firing on both sides, dusk fell, and the whites returned to the fort. Black Hawk then led his eighteen-man party out of what he labeled "this trap," and started home on foot. Five Indians had been killed and several others were wounded in this fight, while the whites had eleven killed and three wounded. The 1815 raids caused so much bitterness that at St. Louis, Clark reported that it might become necessary to destroy "the Rocky River Tribes before we shall have peace."

Soon after the raiders returned to Saukenuk, American authorities demanded that the tribes of the Mississippi Valley make peace quickly and invited the Indians to a grand council at Portage des Sioux that summer. Groups from many tribes attended, but only small delegations from the Rock River villages appeared. Black Hawk claimed that his principal chief, Nomite, decided to attend the council with the Mesquakies as soon as the latter had come back from the lead mines. On the way down the Mississippi, the chief got sick, and the Sauks halted, waiting for him to recover. Instead he died, and his brother, who now became the chief, refused to proceed. Apparently he feared that No-mite's death while en route to the treaty grounds showed that their medicine was bad and that he might also die if he attended the council, so he led most of the Saukenuk contingent home.

Meanwhile the tribal delegations gathered at Portage des Sioux to meet the Americans. The officials brought some $30,000 worth of presents and food for the council and had gathered militiamen from both Missouri and Illinois to accompany the 275 regular army troops there to demonstrate American military strength. That precaution still seemed necessary because many of the warriors radiated confidence in their own prowess, holding the "Americans in great contempt as warriors, little better than Squaws." On July 10, Clark opened the council. He denounced the Rock River villagers' absence and threatened war against them if they failed to arrive within thirty days. Surprisingly, no sooner had the translator finished explaining Clark's comments than the warriors from most of the other tribes leapt to their feet "expressing their assent by vehement cries of applause, which much appaled [sic] the Sacs and Kickapoos." Rumors that the other Indians might attack the delegations from those two tribes circulated freely, so Clark ordered a guard placed around their camps that night. The stern tenor of the governor's remarks and the enmity expressed by the other tribes frightened some of the Sauks at the council grounds, so they set off for home that same night.

Their departure had little impact on the Portage des Sioux Council. The American negotiators continued the talks with leaders of many Mississippi Valley tribes as the summer drew to a close. On September 13, the Missouri River Sauks signed a peace treaty of their own, and by late September the American negotiators prepared to end the council. Fearing continued strife with the Rock River Sauks, they made a last-minute effort to get them to rejoin the negotiations. Governor Clark dispatched agent Boilvin and an interpreter to Saukenuk, but these men failed to persuade the villagers to accept peace. In fact, when the whites reached Saukenuk they found the warriors in the middle of a spirited scalp dance, displaying fresh trophies they had gathered that summer. While Boilvin's report fails to say that he talked with Black Hawk, the ideas he reported hearing were some that the war leader had expressed that year. According to the agent, the Indians suspected that the Americans only wanted them at the Portage des Sioux council so that their tribal enemies could kill them there, and it took Boilvin three days to persuade them otherwise. Although he finally persuaded his listeners to attend the council, the agent's efforts ended in failure because when the Sauks finally reached the meeting ground it was too late. The council had ended two weeks earlier, and the Sauks were told to return the next spring.

American authorities continued to pressure the Sauks to sign a peace accord, while they dispatched another detachment of troops up the Mississippi to build what became Fort Edwards, in Illinois. However, Black Hawk and his fellow villagers ignored the new fort construction and spent that winter in eastern Iowa hunting. The next spring they traveled to St. Louis to meet Clark and negotiate a peace treaty. From the start the meeting went badly. Clark rejected the Sauks' request that they be allowed to keep dealing with the English traders whom they had known for years. Clark's other remarks angered the Indians, and one of the chiefs denounced the Americans as liars. According to Black Hawk, the chief claimed that the Great Father could not have said what Governor Clark reported because the president knew "that the situation in which we [the Sauks] had been placed had been caused by him!" Apparently this referred to the Sauks' understanding that President Madison had promised that they would be able to get their trade goods on credit before their annual hunt each year, when the government traders were expressly forbidden to extend such credit.

Furious at what he understood as an attack on his honesty, Clark threatened to break off the talks and go to war. At that the still-angry chiefs calmed down, and the talks resumed the next day. Neither the American negotiators nor the Indians left any record of what topics the two groups discussed. Yet it seems that Clark and his subordinates had to mix cajolery and threats to get the Sauks to accept a peace agreement because the Indians had defeated the Americans repeatedly during the preceding year. Certainly the whites threatened to withhold access to trade goods, a critical part of the Indian's economy. In addition, once the Rock River villagers realized that the British had deserted them and that all of the other tribes in the Mississippi Valley had already signed peace treaties, they saw little reason to continue the war against the United States in isolation.

As a result, on May 13, 1816, the leaders of the last Sauk villages signed the treaty. Its first article called on the Rock River Sauks to "unconditionally assent to recognize, reestablish, and confirm" the 1804 treaty that had surrendered their Illinois homeland to the United States. One by one the leaders put their marks on the agreement, but later Black Hawk insisted that the Indians still failed to understand its contents because the whites had not explained its provisions clearly. "Here, for the first time," he remarked, "I touched the goose quill to the treaty— not knowing, however, that, by that act, I consented to give away my village. Had that been explained to me, I should have opposed it, and never would have signed their treaty...." Whether true or not, this would remain his explanation of his signature and his later refusal to accept the treaty terms and vacate Saukenuk.

CHAPTER THREE

We were a divided people ◆ 1816–31

Indian hostilities against the United States ended temporarily in the upper Mississippi region on May 13, 1816, when the Sauk and Mesquakie leaders of the Rock River villages signed their treaty with William Clark at St. Louis. Yet many of the causes for the earlier hatred and violence remained unchanged. The tribes wanted to continue their ties with the British traders who had been their friends and economic partners for years. American officials forbade that. With some assurance that Indian raids had ceased, the ever-advancing pioneers accelerated their settlement of central and western Illinois, further disrupting already strained tribal economic patterns. The long-term dispute over the treaty of 1804 and its cession of all Sauk and Mesquakie lands east of the Mississippi remained a source of confusion, misunderstanding, and bitterness between the tribes and American officials. The white's refusal to accept Indian means of restitution for crime and violence also kept both groups resentful and angry toward each other, as the tribal custom of payment of goods or money to the injured party or their surviving relatives found no acceptance within the American legal system.

These issues proved to be only one aspect of Indian difficulties following the War of 1812. The villagers had disputes and problems of their own, matters that affected the whites to a lesser degree than the tribal people themselves. Clearly the wartime experience had shattered tribal cohesion among both the

Sauk and Mesquakie peoples. During 1813 nearly one-half of the Sauks and many Mesquakies had chosen to migrate to Missouri to live out the conflict as neutrals under American protection. True, many of these people had drifted back to the Mississippi and Rock River villages before the war ended, but their earlier moves had demonstrated how little unity existed in both tribes. Some of the divisions grew out of the nature of Indian society itself. Most Sauk people gave their primary allegiance to their own village, not to any larger group. While they recognized some tribal obligations and loyalty, neither the individuals nor the villages necessarily responded to crises as a unit. In fact, the tensions in 1812 between those who wanted to side with the British and those wishing to remain neutral damaged tribal ties permanently. The growing rivalry between Black Hawk and (the younger but more eloquent) Keokuk over military leadership brought dissension and bitterness too.

By 1816, American officials in Missouri and Illinois strove to keep the tribes at peace with each other so that intertribal violence did not harm or frighten the pioneers. Repeatedly delegations of chiefs visiting St. Louis heard Clark's pleas that they settle intertribal disputes short of war. While extending peace, these efforts angered militants within practically every village because they ran directly counter to tribal culture. If the whites imposed peaceful solutions upon Indian disputes, the young men might not be able to gain fame as warriors. An enforced peace would make it impossible to meet family and clan obligations that demanded revenge against enemies and those perceived to have hurt the family or village. So while in theory all the tribes of the region agreed to let the Americans settle their differences short of war, in reality this system was doomed to failure. As a result neither the Indians nor the officials really knew what to expect, and the situation seemed to anger rather than to satisfy everyone. Frontier bureaucrats rarely got all the information they needed to make sense out of the continuing Indian disputes, while tribal civil chiefs had only slight control over the young warriors who caused most of the trouble.

During the decade and a half after Black Hawk first touched "the goose quill to paper," life changed dramatically for the Rock River people. Their isolation vanished quickly, as pioneers poured into Indiana, Illinois, and Missouri. Even before the Sauks and Mesquakies returned from their spring 1816 meeting with Clark, the whites disrupted the villagers' seclusion. In early May 1816, American soldiers landed at Rock Island to begin work on what became Fort Armstrong. The new post, rising virtually next door to Saukenuk, incensed the Indians from the start because it brought troops into their immediate vicinity. The American presence inhibited Sauk actions immediately. Black Hawk voiced the villagers' feelings of betrayal, saying that while the Indians had signed a peace treaty, the whites had begun "to prepare for war in time of peace."

Losing their cherished seclusion was only one reason why the Rock River villagers resented having the troops stationed nearby at Rock Island. They had others. The first was both economic and aesthetic. With its well-drained limestone soil and good water supply, Rock Island had been a favorite summer haunt for Sauk young people for generations. The plentiful bushes and trees supplied blackberries, gooseberries, plums, apples, and nuts, while the nearby streams provided a good supply of fish. These things made the island a pleasant place to hunt, gather, or even picnic. Of equal importance, the island had spiritual significance for the Rock River people. They believed that a good spirit that looked like an oversized white swan lived in a small cave directly under the soldiers' new fort. While enjoying their use of the island, the villagers had carefully avoided making too much noise and inadvertently frightening the spirit. The soldiers, however, had no idea that such a being lived there, and with their noise had driven it away. Black Hawk later complained that with the spirit gone "no doubt a bad spirit has taken its place."

Although invited to meet with the garrison officers and become acquainted, the Saukenuk chiefs refused. Although some of the village leaders complained about the soldiers' presence in their homeland, apparently they had no objections to having both a resident agent and a trader nearby. By 1817 their newly appointed subagent, Thomas Forsyth, had arrived at Rock Island. A veteran trader who understood tribal ways thoroughly, Forsyth worked with the Sauks and Mesquakies for more than the next decade. Although usually effective, even Forsyth had difficulties at times. For example, during the summer of 1817 when he began to issue the annuities to the tribal leaders, the Mesquakie chiefs refused to sign the receipts signifying that they had received the goods. They feared that the papers Forsyth asked them to sign might mean another land cession and told the agent that they "would do without food and live on roots rather than part with their lands" by signing the forms. When the agent explained that the papers had nothing to do with new land cessions and warned the chiefs to take their goods or he would carry them elsewhere, the Mesquakie leaders complied.

At Saukenuk, the village chiefs raised no such complaint, and even Black Hawk took a share of the federal goods that year. Beginning in 1818, however, after learning that the annuities were in payment for the 1804 land cession, he refused to accept any further goods from the government. Instead, he "made a great noise about this land" and denied that Quashquame ever had any authority to sell it to the United States. To avoid being swindled by American negotiators in the future, Black Hawk urged the villagers not to accept any more annuities or presents from the whites lest they later prove to be payments for more land cessions. Convinced that the Americans had lied to and cheated the Sauks, Black Hawk never lost this mistrust.

Although American troops, agents, and traders had moved to Rock Island, many of the Sauks and Mesquakies continued their annual trips to visit the British. Every year from 1816 through 1831 some of these Indians traveled east to Fort Malden to get presents from the British agents. Frequently Black Hawk joined this summer migration. The number of people making the pilgrimage varied widely from year to year, but, with the tribal economy under increasing pressure, for some groups the presents became essential. For example, in 1819 some 340 Sauks received trade goods, ammunition, and food worth approximately $3,400 from the British. The fact that they willingly traveled all the way from the Mississippi to Amherstburg for only $10-worth of goods per person shows how badly their economy had deteriorated that year.

These continuing dealings between the British and the tribal people from the United States brought frequent complaints from American officials. However those men did little to help the Indians themselves. In 1821 some of the Sauks, including Keokuk and Black Hawk, told Forsyth that they had decided not to the make the annual trip to Amherstburg. The overoptimistic agent thought that his actions had weakened British influence among the Sauks. What he failed to realize was that Black Hawk planned to go elsewhere in Canada. Instead of visiting Fort Malden, he traveled farther north to Drummond's Island. There Black Hawk denounced the Americans and boasted that the Sauks feared nobody and that they would fight against the United States any time that it became necessary. He left the island angry, however, because the British refused to give their Indian visitors food and presents anywhere except at Fort Malden.

While Sauk difficulties increased during the immediate postwar years, Black Hawk experienced personal tragedy too. His eldest son died from an unexplained disease. Soon after that his youngest daughter also died. Describing their loss as "a hard stroke," he apparently feared a weakening of his "medicine" and vowed to fast for two years, one for each of the children. Moving the rest of his family out of Saukenuk, he built a lodge in isolation and began a traditional Sauk fast, giving away his property except for a buffalo robe. Then he blackened his face, and virtually stopped eating, having only water at noon and "eating sparingly of boiled corn at sunset." After two years he decided that he had fulfilled his promise to the spirits, so he returned to the village. At that point his remaining family included his wife, two sons, and one daughter.

Had these personal misfortunes been the only difficulties that Black Hawk experienced, the frontier might have remained calm during the postwar era, but still more problems arose for the Sauks and Mesquakies. Their generations-old war with the Osages lost much significance as the two groups encountered new and more dangerous foes after the war. The encroachments of pioneer settlers forced all of the Mississippi Valley tribes to travel farther west each summer for their annual hunts. This brought the Kickapoos, Winnebagoes, Sauks, and Mesquakies into frequent and often hostile contact with the Sioux, who hunted over the very regions the eastern tribes now traversed. Although the Sioux greatly outnumbered any of these other groups, they hunted over a large area, so the Mississippi Valley tribes often had more warriors at any given place than did the Sioux. Still the last thing that the Rock River villagers needed was yet another powerful enemy with whom they had to fight. Although the Sioux provided the young warriors a convenient enemy and a good reason to organize raiding parties each summer, the fighting cost the tribes dearly in casualties and in lost hunting opportunities.

The annual rounds of summer fighting began with a series of Sioux attacks on Mesquakie hunters in Sioux territory, a direct result of Indians responding to the ever-expanding white settlements. When the Mesquakies reacted in 1818, they set off a war that lasted for more than a decade. At that point, Black Hawk was still fasting after the deaths of his two children, but within a year he returned to the warrior's path. Instead of fighting immediately, however, he helped negotiate a conciliatory move that settled differences between the Sauk and Iowa tribes. Making peace with the Iowas allowed the Sauks to join the Mesquakies in the war against the Dakota Sioux, and Black Hawk later boasted of having killed many of these new enemies.

Despite shifting much of their effort to fighting the Sioux, the Sauks and Mesquakies continued to make war on other neighboring groups. Their long-standing feud with the Osages erupted sporadically, and occasionally the Rock River villagers raided them and the Osages' neighbors, the Otoes, who lived along the Missouri River. When they found no enemy camps to raid, some of the warriors turned to robbery and attacks on the thinly scattered frontier population. These actions spurred angry words from the settlers and local politicians who demanded that the federal government either control or move the Indians. Governor Clark misinterpreted the situation completely. He saw the reputed intertribal wars as just a cover for the Indians' real purpose: "to destroy our Traders. . . ." The tribes ignored his threats to halt annuity payments to those responsible for the raids, and the unrest continued.

During the summer of 1820 the warriors killed a Frenchman in one of their forays, so the next year American officials demanded that the chiefs surrender the man responsible for that death. As usual, the Indian leaders claimed that the attackers had left their villages, but they did promise to bring the guilty party to St. Louis later. In June 1821, Sauk leaders revisited Clark and, true to their word, brought two murderers. They also surrendered several Otoe captives whom they had held for some time. Apparently Black Hawk did not accompany the delegation to St. Louis that summer, or, if he did, he played no significant role in the discussions. For his rival, Keokuk, however, this meeting with Clark proved to be of major importance. The American official recognized the Indian leader's potential as a force for peace, and from then on Clark treated Keokuk generously, showering him with praise and presents. Keokuk used his good relationship with Clark to increase his influence within the tribe, in particular at the expense of Black Hawk and the old civil chiefs. When other American officials realized Keokuk's leadership potential, they too worked to help him gain influence. Forsyth noted that short of bad luck, within just a few years the Indian leader's "word among the Sauks and foxes will be their law."

In any contest with Keokuk, Black Hawk's traditional views limited his chances to compete successfully. Although neither man was a hereditary chief and therefore should not have spoken in tribal council meetings or negotiations with the whites, only Black Hawk accepted that prohibition. Keokuk, after his elevation to a war chief, proved a fine orator and did not hesitate to use his skill frequently. In fact, an envious Black Hawk described his competitor as having "a smooth tongue" and being a "great speaker." Still, it took more than talk for Keokuk to gain a position of clear dominance within Sauk society. Gradually he persuaded Clark and his subordinate Forsyth of his need for presents to give to others in the tribe, so the officials gave the rising Sauk leader increased authority over the distribution of annuity goods. Thus, it appeared to the other villagers that their war chief Keokuk was favored by the Americans, and he brought back presents and much needed supplies too. As Keokuk's influence and position among the Sauks rose, those of Black Hawk declined, a phenomenon that frustrated and angered the older warrior but one about which he could do little more than grumble.

While Keokuk solidified his authority, troubles with settlers, soldiers, diplomats, and other Indians continued. A new threat to Sauk peace arose during the early 1820s when American miners demanded access to the lead lands of southern Wisconsin, northwestern Illinois, and eastern Iowa (at Dubuque's mines). The Mesquakies had driven would-be miners from the area a decade earlier, but this failed to stop the pioneers' new surge into the lead-bearing region. In an 1816 treaty, the Ottawas, Potawatomis, and Chippewas (or Ojibwas) had ceded their claims to a part of the lead region to the United States, although those tribes had only a vague title to any of the area. The land there clearly belonged to the Winnebagoes in the north and the Sauks and Mesquakies farther to the south and in Iowa. Despite its questionable claim to the lands, the U.S. government issued leases to miners, and by the summer of 1822, hundreds of pioneers swarmed over the hills near the Fever River in northwestern Illinois and north into southwestern Wisconsin.

The Mesquakie chiefs protested bitterly, echoing Black Hawk's words that they had never sold any of their lands above

the mouth of the Rock River, but to no avail. Their agents, Forsyth at Rock Island and Boilvin at Prairie du Chien, simply announced that the whites had begun mining for lead along the
Fever River. Although the complaints went for naught, Forsyth
at least realized that income from the lead sales was essential to
tribal economic survival. He suggested that the Indians shift all
of their own mining across the Mississippi to the Dubuque area
and thus avoid violent conflicts with the white miners. When
some of the Mesquakies suggested that the United States should
lease a part of the Indian land east of the Mississippi, the officials rejected the idea. Telling them that the land already belonged to the United States and that if they caused any trouble
the government would send troops to settle the issue, the Americans browbeat the Indians into acquiescence. The miners' incursions onto tribal lands continued to provoke violence
throughout the rest of the decade, but it never became a major
issue for Black Hawk.

With the miners to the north and settlers moving toward them
from the south and east, the Rock River villagers faced an unre-
lenting compression of their freedom to travel, hunt, or make
war. By 1821, pioneers had begun moving onto lands south of the
Des Moines River in Iowa, where several Sauk and Mesquakie
bands usually spent their winter hunting season. Again the
chiefs complained bitterly and insisted that they had never sold
the lands in question, and on this issue Keokuk and Black Hawk
cooperated to demand a satisfactory response from the government. They asked Forsyth to write to President James Monroe
for them, hoping to gain a clear understanding of the boundaries of their lands. Forsyth sent the letter as they had asked, but
the officials in Washington failed to respond.

Three years later, during the summer of 1824, continuing Indian complaints persuaded Clark to take another delegation of
Sauks and Mesquakies to Washington: once there, perhaps the
officials would answer the Indians' questions about this latest
boundary dispute. At the same time, the Sioux agent Lawrence
Taliaferro led a group of Sioux leaders from Minnesota to

Washington so that the government would be able to conclude a lasting peace between the Sioux and the Rock River Indians. The Sauks and Mesquakies chose ten of their chiefs, including Keokuk, for the trip. Again Black Hawk remained behind at Saukenuk because he was no chief, only a respected warrior. It seems likely that Keokuk used his influence with Clark to keep his rival off the delegation, but that is only conjecture. Whatever the reason, Black Hawk's absence proved crucial in the later history of both tribes. Had he gone to Washington and seen the size and strength of the United States for himself, it is unlikely that he would have risked war with the Americans. Certainly other Mississippi Valley tribal leaders who visited the capital responded that way. Only those who, like Black Hawk, remained in relative isolation would later prove rash enough to risk war with the United States.

Near the end of June 1824, Clark and his charges left St. Louis for the East. There they met with the Sioux chiefs, but the talks failed to produce an accord between the tribes. After wrangling with their Sioux counterparts, the Sauks and Mesquakies urged American officials to make a settlement of their claims to the northwest tip of Illinois. Keokuk and the other chiefs assured Secretary of War John C. Calhoun that they had no quarrel over past land cessions. Nevertheless, they objected to the government's actions concerning their lands beyond the Mississippi because they had never ceded any territory there. When Calhoun noted that the region in question had been purchased from the Osages, the Sauk leader objected vehemently. Keokuk told Calhoun that the Sauks held title to that land in the same manner that the United States held title to most of its land— through conquest. The Sauks and Mesquakies had taken the land from the Osages, and they saw no reason that the United States should then have the nerve to purchase it from the Osages, who no longer had any right to claim ownership of the tract.

When the talks ended, Calhoun seemed to have accepted Keokuk's views. He promised the chiefs that the government would give each tribe a single payment of $1,000 in cash or goods, ten years of annuities at $500, the services of a blacksmith, some farm implements and cattle, and a few other minor items. After the Sauks accepted the agreement, Calhoun sent Clark and the chiefs to visit several of the major eastern cities. The visitors traveled overland to Baltimore, then to Philadelphia, and on to New York City. After a few days there, they set off for home, impressed with American strength but unable or unwilling to keep the peace in the upper Mississippi Valley.

While the delegation was touring eastern cities, their fellow tribesmen continued to raid the Sioux. By August 1824, Sauk warriors had attacked a Sioux village, and their victims retaliated even before the Sauk chiefs had returned from Washington. Black Hawk's role in the fighting is unclear, but these incidents did little to calm the nerves of Indian office personnel responsible for keeping peace. What the officials feared most was the possibility that pioneer whites might fall prey to marauding bands of warriors, thus touching off a major frontier war. To preclude this, federal officials persuaded the upper Mississippi Valley tribes to put down their weapons and attend a grand council at Prairie du Chien the next summer. There, in 1825, Clark and Lewis Cass, then governor of Michigan Territory, would meet tribes from Minnesota, Wisconsin, Iowa, and Illinois in an attempt to arrange a lasting peace.

Filled with optimism, the commissioners sent messengers to each tribe, and gradually, during the summer of 1825, the Indians filtered into the tiny settlement. By August 1 many delegations had appeared. Chippewas and their bitter enemies the Sioux camped uneasily near each other. Winnebagoes, Potawatomis, Ottawas, and Menominees all put up their lodges while waiting for the festivities to begin. Then on August 4, 1825, the late-arriving Iowas, Sauks, and Mesquakies, made their grand entrance at the council grounds. Apparently conscious that they were the last to arrive and eager to demonstrate their courage and perhaps to intimidate their enemies and rivals, the latecomers put on an exaggerated show of martial activity. Wearing full regalia, when they reached the council site they paddled their war canoes back and forth in full view of the other tribal groups. Chanting and waving their weapons aloft, nearly all the warriors stood in their canoes as they passed the other tribes' lodges. Then, having beached their boats, they marched into the center of the camp, still fully armed and looking ready for war at a moment's notice.

The next day the ceremonies began. In his welcoming speech, Clark explained that the Great Father expected the Indians to settle their differences and reach a lasting peace. He proposed that each tribe describe its claims to hunting territory. Once tribal leaders did that, the commissioners' task seemed clear—they had to persuade the chiefs to keep their hunting parties away from lands that they had agreed belonged to other tribes. In theory this tactic would end the ceaseless warfare and raiding, but in fact the plan had little chance to achieve peace. In their optimism the commissioners overlooked two basic realities of tribal life. First, the custom of personal revenge for real or imagined wrongs permeated the thinking and actions of all the tribes at the council. For the young warriors to renounce such activity was unthinkable, no matter what the whites might demand.

The other issue which Clark and Cass chose to ignore was that for generations the Sauks and Mesquakies had been extending their hunting range farther to the west and into Sioux territory as a direct result of expanding white pioneer settlement. The Sauks' economic necessities would not easily change, so there was little hope that they might stop their territorial expansion at Sioux expense. A similar dispute kept the boundary between the Chippewas of northern Wisconsin and Minnesota and the Sioux in turmoil. So the Sioux found themselves continually squeezed between expanding Chippewas on the north and Sauks and Mesquakies on their southern flank—not a recipe for easy or lasting peace.

The actual negotiations took several weeks, and to no one's surprise, establishing the borders separating the hunting grounds of the Sauks and Mesquakies and the Sioux, and the Sioux and the Chippewas, caused the most-heated discussions. Nevertheless, as the days of August slipped away and the commissioners' supply of food and drink for the Indians dwindled, each tribe came to terms with the whites and its neighbors. On August 19, 1825, the chiefs assembled to hear the results. Alike in principal ways, the treaties bound each tribe to accept certain borders, to cease raids and other acts of revenge against the other tribes, and to allow American officials to settle intertribal disputes. After Clark and Cass read each treaty, the interpreters repeated their words and the tribal leaders filed forward to sign three copies of their respective agreements. Unlike the 1816 Sauk-U.S. negotiations, this time Black Hawk did not sign the treaty and apparently had little influence in the proceedings. After the ceremony, the Indian leaders passed the calumet while some spoke briefly, calling for continued peace and expressing their satisfaction with the proceedings that summer.

Clark, although a veteran in dealing with these tribes, should have known better than to expect the truce signed that summer to last. On the other hand, having succeeded in gathering the tribal leaders together for two weeks of peaceful eating, smoking, visiting, and negotiating may have given him unwarranted confidence. While the bureaucrats ignored or failed to understand that the social demands for clan revenge would doom the treaties, the Indians apparently failed to notice the whites' use of an often-successful tactic. As long as several tribes claimed or used parts of the same region, the government had little chance of buying it. Once the Indians agreed to a particular set of boundaries, however, federal negotiators had to deal with only one set of leaders, and the process of obtaining land cessions became easier. Obviously Clark knew this, and while the council of 1825 failed to assure either whites or Indians a lasting peace, it did speed the process of separating the tribes of the upper Mississippi Valley region from their lands.

The continuing influx of pioneer settlers and miners also helped speed Indian land loss. Often during the 1820s, repeated incidents between pioneers and Indians led to property destruction, theft, insults, and random violence. Roving Indians were a convenient scapegoat when settlers tried to explain the disappearance of cattle and hogs, although inadequate fences and simple carelessness probably caused most livestock losses. Black Hawk himself felt the whites' wrath when he met several pioneers in the woods. They accused him of stealing their hogs and, despite his denial, took his rifle. After firing it, one of the pioneers took off the flint, rendering the gun useless. Then the men attacked, "beating him with sticks" and driving him away from their tiny settlement. Years later he remembered the incident bitterly and complained, "I was so much bruised that I could not sleep for several nights."

His fellow villagers suffered as well. One man cut down a hollow tree inhabited by bees and took the honeycombs back to his lodge for his family. Several frontiersmen followed him back to his home, angrily telling the startled brave that the tree belonged to them and that he had had no right to destroy it. The frightened Indian gave the whites the honey, but that failed to satisfy them. Still angry, they used the hunter's action as an excuse to rob him, and they seized the pack of skins that he had collected during the winter hunt. This left him destitute. He could not pay his debts to the trader and had no way to get food or clothing for his family. When Black Hawk and the other hunters rejoined their bands at Saukenuk, he reported that many of the villagers "complained of similar treatment."

Frontier whites cared little about Indian well-being, and at times seemed to do everything in their power to harm the Native Americans. As settlement began near Saukenuk and whites moved to Rock Island because of the protection Fort Armstrong offered, their contacts with the Sauks and Mesquakies increased rapidly. "We became worse off, more unhappy," Black Hawk noted, because of increased meetings with the whites. The availability of alcohol from the newcomers changed the annual hunting patterns that had taken the Sauks across the Mississippi to live in small hunting camps each winter. Many of the villagers

now chose to hunt near the settlements. This soon caused difficulties because there was little game available in the new areas,
so the hunters' families got less food and fewer trade items than
they were used to getting.

The widespread Indian practice of trading pelts and skins for
alcohol throughout the winter proved to be of more long-term
significance. While the government traders had provided no
credit, they had no alcohol for the Indians either. When private
traders replaced the government factors in 1822, however, they
gave both credit and alcohol to their trading partners. This allowed a rapid increase in the abuse of both items and infuriated
Black Hawk. A bitter opponent of alcohol for most of his life, he
denounced the Indians and whites alike. He raged that often,
having traded away their furs for liquor, the hunters came back
to Saukenuk "in the spring with their families, almost naked,
and without the means of getting anything for them." Because
the extended family helped to feed their destitute relatives, everyone in the entire village suffered.

During the 1820s, then, the Sauk and Mesquakie people witnessed their world collapsing around them. Miners took land to
the north; settlers moved into their hunting areas and disrupted
their claims to the land and its resources. The government's annuities, rarely more than a few hundred dollars a year when
other debts had been paid, did little to help. With their game
now much diminished, their debts growing, and even their
tribal enemies seemingly protected by the American government, the world must have appeared a bleak place. Indeed, their
increasing dependence on alcohol provides one accurate measure of the growing social and economic collapse then occurring
within the villages. Although they had signed treaties of peace in
1825, few tribesmen expected those agreements to last or even
wanted them to do so.

The continuing social and economic breakdown of Sauk society angered Black Hawk and other village leaders. Although
most decided that staying at peace with their tribal neighbors
seemed the best policy, the aging war leader felt otherwise. Early

in 1827, when hunters from the Rock River villages found a large Sioux encampment on the Des Moines River, in direct violation of the 1825 treaty agreement, Black Hawk and John Morgan, or The Bear's Hip, a mixed-blood Mesquakie war leader, called for renewed war. The peace chiefs worked to head off any military actions, but Black Hawk remained adamant in his intention to lead a war party against the hated Sioux. While he met with individuals in his war lodge, Saukenuk civil chiefs came, offering him three horses and other presents to desist. Rejecting their gifts, Black Hawk told them that nothing but his death would prevent him from attacking the Sioux that summer.

This decision reopened the conflict between the sixty-year-old warrior and the peace chiefs and their spokesman Keokuk that had lain dormant for some time. It is impossible to know if Black Hawk called for war merely in order to regain lost stature within the village, but his standing certainly played a part in his intransigence. The peace chiefs tried to isolate Black Hawk when they failed to persuade him to stay at peace. Keokuk and several others reported his war threats to Forsyth at Rock Island, also using this chance to curry favor with the American official. Keokuk and the others agreed to try to dissuade the aggressive Sauk. They also relayed a threat from Forsyth that should the negotiations fail and war parties from the village attack the Sioux, he would demand that the chiefs deliver Black Hawk and the other war leaders to him for transport to St. Louis in chains. If the chiefs could not deliver Black Hawk themselves, the agent said he would have the two thousand American troops stationed near St. Louis sent up the river to take the Sauks by force.

Apparently Black Hawk nursed grievances so deep that neither offers of presents nor threats of military action and imprisonment moved him. The village chiefs made yet another attempt to keep peace, but Black Hawk rejected their offer of seven horses. In late May 1827, Keokuk told the agent that the chiefs had failed to persuade Black Hawk to abandon his plans. Keokuk assured Forsyth that most of the Sauks and Mesquakies favored peace, but admitted that malcontents such as "Black

Hawk and Morgan will [always] find some worthless young men
to follow them." Forsyth then urged the Sioux agent to warn his
charges of a possible Sauk and Mesquakie attack. Forsyth hoped
that the Sioux would end the difficulty by destroying the aggres-
sors so that "not one of any war party from this country may
ever return to their homes." The agent did not get that wish, but
peace came that summer anyway because when Black Hawk
learned that the Sioux had been warned of his intentions, he
thought it unwise to risk an ambush and called off the raid.
Later that summer the Sioux, Mesquakies, and Sauks exchanged conciliatory speeches and ceremonial pipes, so the crisis abated.

That incident illustrates the divergent approaches that Black
Hawk and Keokuk took during the 1820s when facing the difficulties besetting the Sauk people. The older, conservative warrior saw no reason to alter his long-standing Indian practices,
and frequently used traditional arguments and means to protect
what he saw as tribal rights and honor. He certainly wanted no
part of actions that might destroy the Sauk people. His younger
rival, on the other hand, had risen to dominance by choosing to
cooperate with the Americans. Unlike Black Hawk, Keokuk
recognized that traditional means no longer fit the changed situation, so he adopted an accommodationist policy whenever possible in his dealings with the pioneers. In part, Keokuk's
attitude had resulted from his trip east with Clark a few years
earlier. While there he saw the whites' power and numbers, and
after returning to Illinois, he worked to stay at peace with the
Americans. That approach brought Keokuk recognition and
gifts from western officials as they sought to keep the tribe at
peace and to increase his stature within the tribe. During the
Winnebago War of 1827, for example, when Sauk warriors
served as scouts for the U.S. army (the tribe remained neutral),
General Henry Atkinson, who directed the campaign against
the Winnebagoes, gave Keokuk a saddle and a bridle as a personal reward for his cooperation with the army.

Examples of growing American and declining Indian power were numerous during the next few years. In fact, the large and rapid deployment of troops against the Winnebagoes in 1827, that forced the Indians to surrender without the soldiers having to fire a single shot, should have convinced all of the nearby tribes to remain at peace. That it failed to do so shows how dimly they understood their precarious position in the region. During 1827 another incident took place that brought renewed trouble for the Rock River villagers. That summer Illinois governor Edwards demanded that the federal government end the Indian problem by removing all of the tribes from the state. Not only did the governor object to the tribes' holding land in his state, but he also protested their hunting there. The Indians' presence "has been borne by the people for a few years past with great impatience," he grumbled, "and cannot be submitted to much longer."

Federal officials took no immediate action because they saw many demands from frontier politicians calling for Indian removal, and Edwards's complaints had no particular urgency. Governor Edwards, however, refused to let the matter drop. About eight months later he reported some difficulty with the Potawatomis and at that time renewed his insistence that the government get the tribes out of Illinois. This time he threatened that if federal authorities failed to take action the "Indians will be removed, and that very promptly," by the state. Again he got no satisfactory response, but his pressure began to have an effect on the federal authorities who dealt with the tribes. By July 1828 the secretary of war assured Edwards that the federal government would do what he asked. In fact, that official promised that by May 25, 1829, the tribes would move beyond the Mississippi River.

Making that promise to the governor proved far easier than carrying it out. Just a few weeks before the secretary of war agreed to the removal, Forsyth had broached the subject at a Rock Island meeting with Sauk and Mesquakie leaders. When their agent told the chiefs that the government expected them to shift their villages west of the Mississippi, he met a storm of protest. Once again the Indians insisted that they had never sold any of their land north of the Rock River to the United States. Tribal spokesmen asserted that they would never agree to move and desert the bones of their ancestors. Rather, "they would defend themselves against any power that might be sent to drive them from their villages." Forsyth, ever the diplomat, reminded them that Saukenuk lay on the main trail between St. Louis and the lead mines even then being worked by thousands of pioneer miners; as people and supplies moved back and forth over that road, more whites would interfere in their lives, and therefore, he assured the Indians, they would be happier and safer once away from the area. When the delegation rejected Forsyth's advice, he told them not to bother complaining anymore about difficulties with the whites because they had refused to move.

Despite the Indians' anger, the agent felt confident that 1828 would be the last year in which the villagers would recross the Mississippi after their winter hunt. Forsyth was mistaken. Already that summer a minority of Sauk leaders refused to stay in Iowa. Rather, they spoke in a "somewhat insolent" manner and insisted upon returning to Illinois. One Sauk chief, the Red Head, or Mushquetaypay, whom the agent described as a "vile, unprincipled fellow" confronted Forsyth angrily. When the agent told him to remember what he had said in council that day because he might have to repeat it to the authorities later, the Sauk "sneakingly went away without saying a word." It is likely that the chief simply left when he realized that there was little chance of agreement, and that Forsyth had misunderstood his action. Clearly, the Red Head represented a strong dissident faction, at least among the Rock River villagers. Another chief, Bad Thunder, supported this anti-American stand and the well-respected warriors Ioway and Black Hawk did too.

Gradually the opponents of the civil chiefs and a shifting assortment of their followers had come to be known as the British Indians or the British Band. By 1832 Black Hawk's followers had acquired the name British Band, but in 1828 the group included many people who did not follow the aged war leader into battle four years later and who had no serious relationship with the British. In fact, in the early intratribal divisions, Black Hawk seems to have played only a limited role in the debates. Calling him and his followers the British Band in the summer of 1832 only demonstrated American paranoia over frontier problems. Black Hawk never had any serious connection with the British once the War of 1812 had ended. In fact, no clearly identified, insular pro-British group existed over any long period because even Keokuk and some of the civil chiefs had joined in the annual pilgrimages to Amherstburg during the decade following the War of 1812. Each year between 1816 and 1831 some of the Sauks and Mesquakies had visited the British across from Detroit. They saw these whites as just another resource to be exploited, and their visits had little to do with political allegiance and a lot to do with economic dependence. Some years, fewer than one hundred people, including entire families, made the trip east. During particularly bad seasons, several times that many people went to eat British food and enjoy whatever presents might be forthcoming.

As early as the spring of 1828, divisions within the Sauks and Mesquakies led to rumors that some of the British Band planned to start a frontier war against the whites. Whether out of jealousy or fear that such a conflict might actually begin, several Mesquakies hurried to visit Clark in St. Louis to warn him. They made the trip in secret and told Clark that while the Mesquakies would not go to war, they felt less certain about the Sauks. When news of the errand reached the Sauk villages, the chiefs hurriedly sought out the agent to assure him that the rumors had no basis. While protesting their innocence, the tribal leaders denounced the messengers as "idle fellows...who run from place to place telling falsehoods simply to get a few presents." It is even possible that the informers made the trip at the behest of the civil chiefs, who hoped to undermine the influence of Black Hawk and their other tribal opponents. Whatever the reason, spreading rumors of an impending war against the whites did little to ease tensions on the frontier.

That same summer federal officials worked to keep their promise to Governor Edwards that by 1829 they would move all of the Indians out of Illinois. Wherever they met tribesmen, whether at St. Louis, Rock Island, Prairie du Chien, or in their villages, the whites repeated the same theme: the 1804 treaty called for the Indians to give up the land they had sold, and now the government wanted to sell the land to the pioneers. These reports caused much excitement and discussion. "Nothing was talked of but leaving our village," Black Hawk reported. Keokuk and the civil chiefs agreed that they had to move. They "sent the crier through the village" telling the people that they needed to build new villages on the Iowa River rather than returning to Saukenuk after their winter hunt.

That decision angered many of the Indians. The women objected strongly. They would have to clear and break new ground for the summer crops and could not count on good harvests from new fields. Leaders such as the Red Head, Bad Thunder, and Ioway had spoken against leaving the Rock River earlier that summer, and now they met to decide how to respond to the upcoming migration. They questioned Quashquame repeatedly about his understanding of the 1804 treaty, and he still insisted that he never sold any tribal lands north of the Rock River. Satisfied that their fellow tribesman was telling the truth, the opponents of removal coalesced, with Black Hawk taking a leading role in opposing any permanent move west into Iowa.

Apparently the federal officials on the scene had little idea of the divisions their announcement about removal had created. Forsyth, for example, blithely assured Clark that he expected little trouble on this matter. In fact, by July 1828 he told Clark that the discussion over leaving Saukenuk was "now settled among" the Indians. "They will make new villages next Spring," he wrote. As far as the agent knew, the only matter for debate was the location of their Iowa settlements, but he thought that even that matter would be agreed upon before the Sauks left for their winter hunt. He misinterpreted the situation badly.

With the matter still under intense debate among the Indians, the Sauks and Mesquakies crossed the Mississippi for their 1828-29 winter hunt. While there Black Hawk learned that three families of whites had moved into the deserted Saukenuk. The squatters had burned some of the lodges, taken down the Indians' fences, and were quarreling among themselves over their land claims. When he heard this, the aged Sauk traveled ten days back to Saukenuk to investigate. The rumors proved to be true. He even found one family living in his own lodge. Hurrying to Rock Island, he got the interpreter there to write a message to the pioneers. Pointing out that there was plenty of land in the vicinity for them to use, Black Hawk asked that they "not settle on our lands—nor trouble our lodges or fences..." and told them that they had to leave the village "as we were coming back to it in the spring." With this message in hand he visited the whites, but without an interpreter he had no idea what they replied.

Still not satisfied, he returned to Rock Island for a long talk with George Davenport, the resident trader there. Davenport told him the same thing as the other whites—forget about returning to Illinois and move quickly to find a good spot for a new village beyond the Mississippi. Unhappy about that advice, Black Hawk traveled another three days to see the Winnebago subagent at Prairie du Chien. That individual gave him "no better news than the trader had done." Finished talking with the whites, he headed up the Rock River to the Winnebago village led by Wabokieshiek, White Cloud, the Winnebago prophet. A mixed-blood Winnebago and Sauk, White Cloud held considerable influence among the Rock River villages of both tribes. He welcomed Black Hawk and then listened to his version of the dispute. Taking the dissident Sauk's side immediately, White Cloud advised him "never to give up our village, for the whites to plough up the bones of our people." He assured Black Hawk that as long as his people lived peaceably at Saukenuk the government would never bother them, and suggested that he return to the winter hunting camps and persuade Keokuk's followers that they too should return to Saukenuk the next spring. With these words from a man whom Black Hawk held in high regard as a spiritual advisor, the warrior headed back to his camp.

Although the government did not offer the Sauk lands for sale until October 1829, white squatters continued moving into the area. While Article Seven of the 1804 treaty made any effort to settle the lands prior to government sale illegal, generations of pioneers chose to ignore tribal rights and assumed that the government would aid them in any land disputes with the Indians. They therefore squatted on choice parcels of land with the hope that either they would be able to buy the land later at a government auction or force bona fide purchasers to pay them something for improvements. In regions where the Indians had left for good, this process worked moderately well, but at Saukenuk the story was different.

In late winter, as the Sauk hunting groups reunited and began their move toward the Iowa River, where they expected to establish new villages, more white squatters moved into Saukenuk. Most of the civil chiefs had remained west of the Mississippi, but Black Hawk and other dissidents ignored their action. They insisted on returning to the old village, so the chiefs had sent Keokuk along to Saukenuk so that he could speak for them. They hoped that he would persuade many of the villagers to return to the new camps on the Iowa River and to prevent any trouble between Black Hawk and the intruding pioneers. With the Watchful Fox and the whites keeping them under close surveillance, the dissidents turned to rebuilding or repairing their lodges and fences. The women had to find small patches of ground still unclaimed by the squatters in which to plant corn and other crops, while the men hunted and fished.

Keokuk remained at the village and repeatedly urged the Sauk there to leave, but few took his advice. Instead they continued to plant new crops. Black Hawk and the other leaders considered Keokuk just another troublemaker, and they blamed him for having failed to get them permission to stay at Saukenuk. Not only did Black Hawk and Keokuk consider each other rivals, but now they also represented opposing views of the Sauk future. Each side in this internal dispute worked to ensure the survival of Sauk identity. Black Hawk and the other traditionalists assumed that in order to keep the heart of the tribe alive, the Indians had to retain Saukenuk with its ancestral graves and the accompanying annual ceremonies they had shared. Keokuk and his supporters saw a need to accommodate the Americans to prevent them from destroying the people. They had been east to Washington, some of them more than once. They knew of the size and strength of the government and had at least some vague idea about the white population. The traditionalists had no such knowledge. They still talked of defeating the militiamen on the Mississippi River during 1814 and saw no reason why patriotic Sauk warriors might not repeat those earlier victories.

Black Hawk feared and disliked Keokuk. Noting that their friendship had ceased, he denounced his opponent as "a coward, and no brave, to abandon his village to be occupied by strangers." Keokuk and the civil chiefs he represented had accepted the inevitability of losing their Rock River lands, while Black Hawk clung to a hope that the tribe could retain them. In terms of strict legality, Black Hawk's stand was correct. The Indians still had the right to live at Saukenuk until it had been sold, and the treaty made the government responsible for keeping the pioneers away (though it did not). While Forsyth and the garrison commander at Fort Armstrong admitted that the Indians had legitimate complaints, they claimed they lacked the authority to oust the squatters from the village. All they did was listen, express sympathy, and urge the Sauks to leave before things got worse.

About the only thing upon which Keokuk and Black Hawk agreed was the need for the Indians to avoid any incidents that might give the whites an excuse to use force against them. When the squatters refused to keep their cattle out of the Indians' corn patches, Keokuk asked them to corral the animals. One of the whites refused, so the Indians turned the pioneer's animals into his own corn fields at night, and the problem ended, at least for a time. During the summer other incidents strained the patience of the Indians and the nerves of the whites. Several times when hungry Sauk women took green corn to eat, the pioneers beat them. When a young man opened a fence the whites had run across the road into the village to let his horse through, several of the squatters beat him so badly that he soon died. Other whites openly sold whiskey throughout the village, got the Indians drunk, and "cheated them out of their horses, guns, and traps." This was too much for Black Hawk, who had counseled nonviolence toward the interlopers all summer. He asked the whiskey vendors to halt their sales, and most quit. Joshua Vandruff, however, refused, so Black Hawk and a small party of warriors smashed his whiskey barrels. The Sauk said that he destroyed the whiskey "for fear that some of the whites might be killed by my people when drunk."

Leaders of the dissidents also visited agent Forsyth at Rock Island to complain about the squatters' actions. At one of these meetings Quashquame again claimed that when he signed the treaty in 1804 he had not been told that it included any land north of the Rock River. Forsyth reminded him that he, and Black Hawk too, had signed a second treaty in 1816, one that specifically accepted the earlier land cession. Hearing this, Black Hawk denied that the whites had mentioned any cession during the 1816 talks. He accused the American negotiators of saying one thing to the Indians and then putting something else on paper. If the 1816 treaty had any clause regarding Sauk lands at the Rock River in it, he said that the Indians had not been told of such a statement or that the whites had added it secretly.

At this the angry Forsyth stopped the discussion. A few days later the Sauks returned for another talk with the agent. This time their frustration became obvious. The dissidents denounced the government, asserting that they would never leave

their village and that they would defend their homes until they died. Everything these Indians said and did at the time indicates that they believed that they had not sold the Rock River lands and that the Americans had, in fact, lied to them ever since the signing of the 1804 treaty. As a result, they seethed with self-righteous anger at being pushed from their homes by violent, cheating intruders. That perception never wavered and kept tribal divisions and unrest at a near fever pitch for the next several years.

Having talked in vain to their agent and the commanding officer at Fort Armstrong, Black Hawk tried to get visiting dignitaries to help. When former Illinois governor Edward Cole and the writer James Hall stopped at the fort, the aging Sauk appealed to them for help. Even after Cole told him that he no longer held any political office or power, Black Hawk insisted on explaining the situation. He repeated the story about Quashquame's denial and added that he had never known the old chief to lie. Then he complained that squatters had taken Indian land, burnt their lodges, fenced their fields, and made the villagers drunk, while the Indian agents refused to help prevent any of those activities. Hall later wrote about the incident and remembered that Black Hawk had recounted the villagers' difficulties with the whites graphically. "We dare not resent any of these things," the Sauk told his listeners. "If we did, it would be said that the Indians are disturbing the white people and troops would be sent out to destroy us." Neither the former governor nor Hall could do anything but express their sympathy.

With fall coming the Saukenuk residents prepared for their winter hunt beyond the Mississippi. Black Hawk made one last stop to talk with Forsyth, hoping that the agent might finally have good news for his dispirited companions. Not only did the agent have nothing encouraging to say, but he told the Indians that the land at Saukenuk would go on sale on the third Monday in October. Once the villagers' former lands had been sold to individual citizens, the Sauks would have no right to live there or even to hunt on the east side of the Mississippi. Forsyth told the

Indians that if they "returned next spring" they "would be forced to remove." With this news the last legal right the villagers had to the lands at the mouth of the Rock River ended. Black Hawk and other Sauks of his generation now had to leave the only permanent home they had ever known.

When the disconsolate Sauks moved west to begin their 1829 winter hunt, the civil chiefs, white squatters, and frontier officials all must have breathed a sigh of relief. Everyone hoped that the stubborn remnant from Saukenuk would join their friends and relatives in the villages along the Iowa River and that Indian-white difficulties in western Illinois had ended. This did not occur. The tribal council had given Keokuk the responsibility of persuading the Sauk holdouts to stay west of the Mississippi, and although he had spent the entire summer of 1829 trying to achieve the chiefs' goals, he had failed. In late 1829 Keokuk threw up his hands in despair. "If any Indians did attempt to return to reside at Rocky River next spring," he said, "they must take their chance."

As the Indians headed west, federal land office officials in Springfield held the advertised October 1829 sale of Sauk lands. Few pioneers bought the land at Saukenuk, but the trader George Davenport purchased about three thousand acres there. During the 1829–30 winter, Black Hawk responded to his action angrily. "The reason was plain to me, why he urged us to remove," he noted bitterly, "His object, we thought, was to get our lands." The irate Indians met repeatedly trying to decide what they should do, and despite everything they had been told the preceding summer, they chose to return to Saukenuk the next spring. During some of the more-heated discussions, the Sauks talked of killing Davenport, Clark, Forsyth, Antoine Le-Clair the interpreter, the commanding officer at Fort Armstrong, and Keokuk. Of the people on their potential death list, the "trader stood foremost" because he had actually bought the land out from under them.

When the Indians denounced Davenport for having bought their lands, he claimed that he had purchased them in an effort

to help the tribe; after all, he reasoned, if he had not bought the land someone else would have done so. He then offered to help the Sauks negotiate a trade of other lands for their village site if the government would accept such a swap. It is not clear if Davenport was being honest with the Indians or not. If the Indians remained near his trading post on Rock Island he would enjoy a more successful trade than if they moved to Iowa. Still, it seems likely that he expected the region to fill with settlers soon, so, having the capital, he invested it in prime land. In any case, his protestations satisfied Black Hawk, and the villagers seem to have forgotten about murdering the whites whom they blamed for their troubles.

The winter of 1829–30 proved difficult for all of the Sauks and Mesquakies in Iowa. Poor hunting and rigorous weather caused much suffering, and members of the rebellious band convinced some of Keokuk's followers to join them in their return to the Rock River in the spring. Despite the defections, tribal leaders refused to have anything to do with the movement. Among those who chose to disobey the dictates of the tribal council and to ignore the warnings of the American officials, the women played a major role. They kept the family garden patches and did most of the farm work. In talking with those who had begun the task of clearing fields at the new villages, the other women learned how difficult the work was and had no desire to face the same struggle if it could be avoided. Therefore they spoke in favor of returning to their Rock River fields where they could work the rich, well-tilled soil, assured of good crops. Some of the men may have favored the return just to show their displeasure with the tribal leaders for giving in to the whites too easily or to show their independence from the Sauk council.

By the spring of 1830, Black Hawk realized that there was no way to expel the whites from the village, but nonetheless his determination to return to the Rock River remained strong. Now in his mid-sixties, the aging warrior saw the end of an era. Black Hawk thought of himself as a personification of traditional Sauk values, and throughout his narrative of these events he stressed

the need to act as a brave or in a manner that brought honor to the tribe. His bitterness at Keokuk and the civil chiefs stemmed from their willingness to abandon the village "merely for the good opinion of the whites." Labeling that action "cowardly," he rebelled at the idea of being forced from the site. Not only was it where he and many of the others had spent most of their lives, but also, and more important, the nearby graves contained "the bones of many friends and relatives," including those of his parents and two of his children. Asserting that he felt a "sacred reverence" for the village site, he insisted that he could never consent to leave it unless removed forcibly.

The year before, Black Hawk and the other Rock River leaders had hoped to be able to go to Washington to present their case to the president. By early 1830 they realized there was no chance for that, so they adopted a legalistic stand based on the 1804 treaty. They understood that the government could force them to leave the lands it had sold, but those represented only a portion of the village site, and Davenport owned that area. The rest of the land remained unsold, although squatters held some of it. The Sauks claimed the right to use the remaining land under their treaty. Seeking advice from new sources, Black Hawk traveled east to discuss these matters with the British officials at Fort Malden. There he heard the same thing that the British had been saying for a decade. They told him to go to Washington and speak with the president, who would treat the Indians fairly. On his way back to Illinois, the aging Sauk and his companions stopped in the Michigan Territory to talk with Governor Cass. He assured the group that if they had not yet sold their lands they could remain on them and that as long as they remained at peace, the government would not disturb them.

While the new opinions may have made Black Hawk and his friends feel better about their situation, whatever hope they derived from them proved to be ill-founded. The advice was good, if the Sauks had not sold the lands in question, but, as far as the government was concerned the debate had ended because the Indians themselves had recognized the land cession in several

ways: the tribal council had accepted the 1804, 1815, and 1816 treaties as valid agreements, although they complained that the government had not been clear about what was being sold or some of the other terms; as early as 1829 even Black Hawk had based his objections to the squatters at Saukenuk on the treaty, claiming that the Indians had the right to live there until the government actually sold the land. Still, the parleys with the British had given the Sauks a new thread of hope. More important, they had convinced Black Hawk that he was right, and therefore the villagers could remain at Saukenuk.

Late in the fall of 1830, Black Hawk returned to Saukenuk, but the Sauks there had already scattered for the winter hunt, so he followed. At the village the Indians had endured much trouble from the squatters during Black Hawk's absence; also their small hunting camps had suffered another poor season, and the Sauk leaders conferred repeatedly around the flickering campfires. They sent messengers to seek advice from White Cloud (Wabokieshiek) the Winnebago prophet. Several of the chiefs decided that some direct action was imperative and that winter set out to visit tribes on the Arkansas, and Red rivers, and beyond into Texas. This group included Black Hawk's eldest son Whirling Thunder or Nasheweskaka; Namoett, recognized as one of two chiefs of the British Indians; Ioway, one of the most anti-American warriors; and several others. The exact purpose of this delegation remains uncertain.

Black Hawk said only that the group had gone west on a secret mission not related to the dispute over Saukenuk. Rumors at the time suggested that the whites feared that the Sauks were passing war messages to each tribe they visited, hoping to recruit allies for a new war. It seems more likely that they sought a future refuge and merely visited the other tribes in an effort to see if any of them might allow the embattled Sauks to move into their country. Whatever their mission, the Indians' travels that winter failed to change their situation. No new allies appeared, and apparently no tribes or villages volunteered any part of their territory for the Rock River people. Yet the journey proved im-

portant for a different reason. While returning from Texas during the spring of 1831 both Namoett and Ioway died. This
removed some of the recognized dissident leaders and allowed
new, younger chiefs to assume positions of leadership. While
they might have more vigor than their more mature predecessors, they also lacked the experience necessary to lead well during turbulent times. In any event, during the spring of 1831, even
before news of the deaths reached the hunting camps, Black
Hawk and the others had returned to Saukenuk.

While these Indians had agonized, debated, and argued over
what course of action they should take during the preceding several years, other events in the Mississippi Valley altered the situation there substantially. During the summer of 1828, Morgan
quarreled with the head chiefs at the Dubuque village. Angry at
what he considered their unwillingness to defend Mesquakie
rights in dealing with the whites and the Sioux, he led a war
party in an attack against the latter. Hoping to avoid Sioux retaliation, Mesquakie and Sauk leaders surrendered a woman
taken captive in the raid, but failed in their efforts to recover her
young daughter. Because neither the tribal leaders nor the agent
could persuade the Sauk family that held the child to return her,
peace remained in doubt.

The continuing unrest and bad feelings between the Sioux
and their enemies to the south disrupted the fur trade in the region and threatened to plunge the entire area into renewed war.
The fur traders complained to the government, seeking help to
keep their business going. At the same time, continuing pressure from pioneer settlements forced the people of the Mississippi Valley to travel farther west to hunt each year and brought
armed young men from several tribes into repeated and dangerous contact with the Sioux. During 1829 a Sauk and Mesquakie
war party killed sixteen Sioux, and families of the victims called
for retaliation. So, once again, despite the fact that most Sauk
chiefs called for peace, they had little control over those in their
villages who chose to carry out raids.

Clark and his subordinates realized that they once again had
to intervene in order to break the cycle of raids and counter-

raids, so they tried to act as pacifiers by having the government make payments to "cover the dead." Recognizing that money spent on presents for the survivors of hostile attacks would be far less expensive than renewed frontier warfare, and that some of the continuing raiding had resulted from the government's failure to carry out the promises made to the tribes under the 1825 treaties, officials made arrangements to hold another council at the end of the summer of 1830 at Prairie du Chien. There they expected to get agreements to end the raiding and to commit the federal government to paying the costs of covering the dead on both sides.

Not only did their efforts to bring about this new peace initiative fail, but they fed the flames of anti-American feelings among the Indians. In late March 1830, Clark invited Sauk and Mesquakie leaders to St. Louis. There they discussed previous treaties, Indian dissatisfaction with the 1825 boundaries, and complaints of Sioux incursions. The Indians pressed Clark for a chance to present their grievances to the president, but without success. Instead, Clark persuaded them to meet the Sioux, Winnebagoes, and Menominees at Prairie du Chien for another round of negotiations. The Indians found little to their liking in Clark's message and left for home with the matter unsettled.

Had this been the end of federal actions before holding a treaty council, little more would have happened. However, following orders from the secretary of war, the new subagent at the Fever River, Wynkoop Warner, called for Mesquakie leaders from Dubuque to meet with him and the Sioux, Winnebagoes, and Menominees to accept a truce in order to allow serious negotiations to be held later that summer. The agent notified the northern tribes that the Mesquakies would come to parley while sixteen of the Mesquakie village leaders, one woman among the party, started up the Mississippi by canoe. On the evening of May 5, 1830, the delegation landed to prepare camp for the night when about fifty Sioux, Winnebago, and Menominee warriors stormed the camp. Because the Mesquakie mission was to seek peace, they carried no weapons and so could not protect themselves when their enemies attacked. The attackers killed all but one man, a part-Winnebago, and sent him back to the Mesquakie village to tell what had happened. Ironically all of the leaders who died in the ambush had favored peace. Only John Morgan, whose rash action two years earlier had reopened the war, had not joined the delegation, so the Dubuque villagers' only remaining leader proved to be the one most eager for war.

As soon as they learned of their leaders' deaths, the Mesquakies fled south, to just across the river from Fort Armstrong, and appealed to their other villages and the Sauks for help. The tribal councils gave Katice, a leading Mesquakie chief, authority to lead a war party as some five hundred men from the two tribes prepared to launch a counterattack. Fortunately, Forsyth urged calm and persuaded them to visit Clark before making their attack. Some 213 Indians, including many chiefs, took his advice, jamming into every corner of Clark's council chamber. The Indians complained bitterly, and Keokuk blamed the American officials for the tragedy because chief Peahmuska and the others had been lured to their deaths by the agent's call. The Indians rejected Clark's call for a parley with the northern tribes at Prairie du Chien. Keokuk warned his listeners that "I can't shake hands with the Sioux and Menominees, until we are paid for covering our dead." Despite the Indians' adamant objections, Clark eventually persuaded them to attend the forthcoming peace talks, but that took yet another meeting in St. Louis and the distribution of $1,000 in gifts to temporarily soothe anger over Sioux treachery. Clark also succeeded in removing nearly one hundred squatters who had moved onto the Mesquakie lead lands at Dubuque immediately after the villagers had fled south.

Later that summer reluctant Sauk and Mesquakie leaders traveled north to Prairie du Chien to meet their enemies. The federal officials held councils for a little more than a week, persuading the tribesmen to agree to peace. While he had the tribal leaders together, Clark again tried to acquire parts of their land. He asked the Mesquakies to sell their mineral lands at Dubuque, but by this time they recognized how valuable those lands had become and demanded a fair price (far higher than the government offered). Despite this failure, Clark succeeded in getting several of the tribes to sell more of their territory between the Mississippi and Missouri rivers, which was then to be divided into clearly defined hunting territories for the Indians in the area. The small contingent of Sauk and Mesquakie leaders agreed to accept a ten-year annuity of $6,500 for their territorial concessions.

Had the peace agreement held and the tribes stopped their attacks against each other, these incidents would have played little role in Black Hawk's life during 1831. Instead, the Mesquakies reopened the Sioux war that next summer. Because of long-standing Indian custom, the relatives of murdered persons were the sole judges of the adequacy of payments to cover the blood of the dead. Accordingly when some of them decided that the 1830 treaty payments failed to adequately cover the blood of their kinsmen, they called for war. This was a cultural imperative that none could avoid, and in August 1831, a Mesquakie and Sauk war party killed a group of twenty-five Menominees near Prairie du Chien, destroying the hard-won peace agreement. American officials now feared that the gifts they provided to the families of the Menominee victims to cover the blood of their dead might also be rejected (as the Mesquakies had done) and that full-scale war would soon erupt. To forestall that, the war department ordered General Atkinson to call the Mesquakie leaders to Rock Island for a council. Atkinson was to demand the surrender of those responsible for the attack on the Menominees, to take hostages, and to threaten war if the fighting did not cease. This action pushed those culturally conservative Mesquakies who had supported the retaliatory attack and their leaders into Black Hawk's camp by 1832, thus strengthening the Sauk's determination to resist a complete withdrawal from Saukenuk that summer.

With these events swirling around them, the Sauks and Mesquakies remained bitterly divided over whether or not to cooperate with American officials (to stay on the Iowa River rather than return to Illinois). Despite the repeated efforts of the civil chiefs, traders, agents and their interpreter to keep the Sauks west of the Mississippi, in the spring of 1831, Black Hawk and his companions decided to return to Saukenuk. News of their action sped to Illinois governor John Reynolds, who demanded that the federal government get the Indians out of his state once and for all. He wrote Clark that he had issued a call for seven hundred mounted militiamen to move these Indians "dead or alive" to the west side of the Mississippi. When General Gaines heard of Reynolds' action, he assured the governor that he had plenty of troops to deal with the Sauks and that, for the moment, he considered the militia force unnecessary. Then he ordered ten companies of regular infantrymen north to Fort Armstrong.

At Saukenuk, the men repaired and rebuilt their lodges while the women began planting a new crop of corn. The squatters living nearby wanted no part of having the Indians as neighbors, and as soon as the Indians' corn came up the squatters started to plow up the Indians' garden patches. Black Hawk and other Sauk leaders told the whites that they had to leave, apparently threatening them if they remained after the next day. Surprisingly, most of the troublemakers fled, and, temporarily, it appeared as if the villagers might have an uneventful summer. They hunted and fished nearby, and even held some of their tribal ceremonies and games. During what seemed the most pleasant season they had experienced in Illinois for several years, they learned that the "great war chief," General Gaines, was even then on his way up the Mississippi with a large number of troops. Hurriedly Black Hawk traveled to the White Cloud's village for advice. There the Winnebago mystic told his visitor that he had dreamed that Gaines only wanted to frighten the British Band people into leaving the village. "He assured us," Black Hawk reported, "that this 'great war chief dare not, and would not, hurt any of us.'" The prophet encouraged the British Band to refuse any offer the General made to them.

With those recommendations still in his ears, Black Hawk headed back down the Rock River to the village. There the regular troops arrived on June 3, and the next day Gaines called the chiefs together. Much to Black Hawk's displeasure, Gaines made certain that the leading civil chiefs of both the Sauk and Mesquakie tribes attended the council. The old warrior and his followers arrived at the meeting place in full war regalia, chanting and singing while they brandished their weapons. When the noise quieted, Gaines relayed the president's anger that the Indians had not stayed west of the Mississippi. He reminded them that although they had fought against the United States and had continued to act unfriendly toward its people, the government had always treated them civilly. Then he reviewed the treaties of 1804, 1816, and the more recent 1825 agreement signed at Prairie du Chien and told the Indians that they had no choice: they had to remain west of the Mississippi!

Quashquame, apparently the highest ranking chief among the Rock River band, responded as he had so often on other occasions. No matter what the treaties said, he denied that he ever sold the land north of the Rock River. The general replied that he had no part in writing the treaties, but that he had orders to move the villagers across the river. Then Black Hawk stood. Striding forward, he told Gaines that the braves with him were "unanimous in their desire to remain in their old fields; they wish to harvest their corn and will do so peaceably. . . ." At this Gaines asked "who is the Black Hawk that he should assume the right of dictating to his tribe?" The old warrior sat down for a moment. Then he stood again and replied angrily that he was a Sauk like his ancestors. "They have left their bones in our fields, and there I will remain and leave my bones with theirs," he said. At that point Gaines ended the meeting abruptly, telling his listeners to think about their decision until the next day.

During the night Keokuk and the civil chiefs moved through the lodges urging people to leave before any fighting began. By morning they had convinced about fifty families to abandon Saukenuk, and Keokuk told Gaines that he expected more would eventually join the rest of the tribe in Iowa. He pleaded that no hostile action be taken until the civil leaders could get people across the river and out of harm's way. At the same time, he complained that the soldiers at Prairie du Chien had not prevented roving bands of Sioux warriors from attacking Sauk and Mesquakie hunting parties in Iowa and urged that the troops be used more effectively. Then he noted that if all the Rock River villagers crossed west to Iowa without being able to harvest their crops that some might starve there during the next winter. Therefore he asked Gaines for corn to feed the refugees that winter. Gaines agreed to provide food after the last of the Sauks moved west.

Meanwhile, Black Hawk and his companions avoided Gaines's camp that day and the next. On June 7 Black Hawk's group appeared, this time leading an old woman who claimed that her father had been a chief friendly to the United States. She had never heard him say that any of the Sauks had sold the village site, so that must not have happened. Then she asked for time for the crops to mature so that the women could harvest what they had planted. "And, if we are driven from our village without being allowed to save our corn," she told the General, "many of our little children must perish with hunger!" Black Hawk later reported that Gaines told the woman that President Jackson had "not sent him here to make treaties with the women, nor to hold councils with them!" Dejectedly the Sauks left the fort, returning to their village for more deliberations. Later that day they again proposed that they be allowed to stay until the corn harvest. Gaines sent a curt reply. They had three days to cross the Mississippi or he would use his troops to drive them into Iowa.

Despite his threats, Gaines hesitated to begin an Indian war, and he waited cautiously at Fort Armstrong. He learned that a small delegation of Kickapoos, Winnebagoes, and Potawatomis had visited the Rock River village, as had the prophet White Cloud, and this made Gaines pause. Black Hawk had promised only nonviolent resistance, but the officers feared treachery. In addition, the extra troops that Gaines had ordered to descend the Mississippi from Forts Winnebago and Crawford had not yet arrived. Therefore the soldiers kept a tense watch on the Indians, who professed little fear of the army and repeated their determination to remain at the village. Then on June 25, 1831, Governor Reynolds arrived at the head of 1,400 militiamen. Now Gaines could act. He directed the armed steamboat *Winnebago* to move up the Rock River and placed his artillery near the village. When the Sauk spies reported that the militia columns were only a few miles from Saukenuk, the Indians reconsidered. Dealing with the well-disciplined regulars was one thing, but Black Hawk reported that he "was afraid of the multitude of pale faces, who were on horseback, as they were under no restraint of their chiefs." Realizing that to remain at the village invited disaster, the Sauks broke camp and fled across the Mississippi that same night. In the morning when the troops stormed through the village they found dying fires and an old dog.

The next day, Sauk leaders received word from General Gaines that they should come to Rock Island for another council. The civil chiefs and Keokuk appeared, but Black Hawk and those with him refused to recross the river. At this Gaines threatened to lead his troops against the dissidents unless they cooperated. After considerable urging by Keokuk, the leaders of the British Band agreed. On June 30, 1831, they beached their canoes on Rock Island and marched up to Fort Armstrong to meet the general. As they sat in the meeting room one of the officers read the terms of the "Articles of Agreement and Capitulation" written by Gaines and Reynolds. After each line LeClair translated what had been read. The document called for the British Band and its leaders to submit to the authority of Keokuk and the tribal civil chiefs. They were to remain west of the Mississippi at all times, stop traveling to Canada to get presents from the British, and allow the government the right to build military posts and roads in their country west of the Mississippi.

When Lieutenant George McCall, the general's aide, finished reading the agreement and all of its terms had been translated, the ceremony continued. McCall waved Quashquame forward to sign the document as the principle chief of the British Band. He made his mark. Then came Black Hawk's turn. Without a word the aged warrior stood and moved forward with a measured tread. Years later Lieutenant McCall reported that "deep-seated grief and humiliation" crossed his face as he came up to the table. There he took the quill pen, and when the officer pointed to the place he was to mark, the Sauk made a "large bold cross with a force that rendered that pen forever unfit for further use." As the others watched silently, he turned and strode back to his seat. Black Hawk remembered this day clearly. "I touched the goosequill to this treaty," he reported, "and was determined to live in peace."

Although Black Hawk never recorded his reasons for signing this agreement, several seem apparent. If the Saukenuk people were to survive the next winter in Iowa they needed corn from the government: they could no longer expect to harvest a crop that year. In addition, General Gaines commanded a powerful force of regular army troops, and the Indians had no desire to provoke open combat under those circumstances. Repeatedly, the aging warrior had said that he would never voluntarily abandon the village in Illinois, but he had no death wish either. Now he could say that he had led the tribal resistance to forced removal beyond the Mississippi, and that tribal efforts to remain in Illinois had failed. The force of events gave the Sauks no alternative to removal other than destruction, and Black Hawk's goal was to preserve Sauk existence, not destroy it. Having done his best to stem the tide of invading whites, he could now accept the inevitable and agree to stay in Iowa. Unfortunately, he did not stick to his resolve.

CHAPTER FOUR

My object was not war ◆ 1831–32

With the forced removal of the Sauk and Mesquakie tribes west to Iowa completed during the summer of 1831, Black Hawk appeared to have prepared himself for a quiet retirement. Because the tribal agreements with the United States included promises of agricultural assistance, Black Hawk asked the Iowa agent to have a small log house built and some land plowed for him that autumn. Felix St. Vrain, the agent, agreed, probably figuring that at last the old troublemaker would stay out of tribal affairs. Black Hawk also asked Davenport if he could be buried in the village graveyard which was on the trader's land. Davenport agreed readily to this. So it indeed looked as if the aging warrior, now about sixty-five, actually would cease causing problems for the American officials conducting Indian affairs in the Mississippi Valley. Instead, the various discontents of individual Indians and disaffected groups within several tribes all came together during the summer of 1832 and caused what became known as the Black Hawk War.

No sooner had the last of the Sauks begun to settle down in Iowa than renewed troubles began. Reports circulated that some of the Illinois militiamen had torn open Indian graves, exhumed some of the remains, and even burned some bones. Hearing this, a few of the warriors returned to rebury their dead or their remains, only to be driven off by the pioneers. Then, still that same autumn, the corn that General Gaines had provided to feed the villagers began to run out. With their children crying from hunger and their wives grumbling that they do something, some of the Indian men slipped back across the Mississippi to harvest a bit from their corn and melon fields. Once again, the local whites drove the Indians off with gunfire. To the frustrated Indians, these incidents made it seem that the whites hoped to starve them and kept alive the anger and bitterness that some of the Sauks and Mesquakies felt toward the Americans.

These tribal people saw their traditional ways nearing collapse. Keokuk and most of the civil chiefs chose to accept American offers of help in exchange for altering their lifestyle. Those who rejected that approach came together to form the British Band. Usually identified as Black Hawk's followers, this group included a variety of disaffected people. Sauks, Mesquakies, Kickapoos, Winnebagoes, and a smattering of other people composed the band membership. The very existence of such a polyglot group of people demonstrates the snowballing collapse of tribal society at the time. Indians had always moved freely from one village to another, but usually they remained connected firmly to existing bands or clans and accepted the leadership of recognized chiefs and warriors. Among the Sauks and Mesquakies these customs had begun to founder as their lives became ever more difficult and unpleasant.

The reemergence of the British Band, then, resulted from many small actions and events, not some carefully thought-out plot to bring violence and despair to the Illinois frontier. As was mentioned, the label attached to Black Hawk's followers had been used sporadically for several decades because some of the Indians had sided with the British during the War of 1812. It remained in use later because many Sauks and Mesquakies visited British officials at Fort Malden or at Drummond's Island almost every year. (Although Indians from many tribes near the Great Lakes did the same thing, they did not acquire the epithet.) Nevertheless, American officials suspected that British agents in Canada manipulated their tribal visitors into taking anti-American actions, or at least anti-American attitudes, because of the annual gifts they provided. The Indians saw the gifts as the friendly gesture of a former ally, and they hoped that the British might advise and help them in their dealings with the United States. In any case, many reasons existed for the evolution of a new band comprised mostly of Sauks and Mesquakies and the subsequent labeling of this group as the British Band.

During the summer and autumn of 1831, several events occurred that kept the situation unsettled for the Indians. Sometime near the end of the summer, Bad Thunder, one of the principle Sauk chiefs among the dissidents, died. Then, shortly after signing the surrender agreement made with General Gaines, the Mesquakie Morgan also died. The deaths of these two men, when added to those of Namoett and Ioway during the preceding year, brought major shifts in leadership among the British Band. By midwinter of 1831–32, a new, younger, and less experienced group of chiefs emerged. Lacking the caution of their predecessors and having only modest respect from their followers because of their relative youth, these men tended to look for advice to the few old warriors still willing to play an active role in village life. Under these conditions it was only a matter of a few months until they enticed Black Hawk out of his self-described retirement.

The new leadership developed in a situation of near political vacuum and general despair among the people that autumn. Even before General Gaines had forced the Indians from Saukenuk the preceding summer, Napope, a young chief and the only regular member of the Sauk tribal council among the British Band leadership, had left to visit the British at Fort Malden. Bitterly unhappy at what he considered American mistreatment, Napope had urged support of the plan to kill Clark, Forsyth, the interpreter, the trader, and the commanding officer at Fort Armstrong: in fact, he had threatened to kill several of those men himself. At Fort Malden, Napope brought the Sauks' view of their problems with the United States to the attention of the British agents. Whatever those men told him, when the young chief returned from Canada he reported that a British of-

ficial had promised that "they would stand by and assist us" if a
war with the Americans began. Of course, the British had told
him no such thing. Rather they had urged the Indians to remain at peace since 1815, when hostilities with the United States
ended.

Napope's report helped stir unreasonable expectations
among his fellow tribesmen, as did reports of some of the visions
that the Winnebago prophet had seen. White Cloud had considerable influence over people in the British Band. A mystic and
religious teacher, he dreamed or saw visions and advised Black
Hawk and others when they asked for help. Not quite as young
as Napope, probably in his late thirties, White Cloud became a
significant force in the 1832 Sauk return to Illinois. He lived at a
small village of perhaps two hundred people, some thirty to
forty miles up the Rock River from Saukenuk. He preached a
return to Indian moral values and a separation from the whites
whenever possible. When asked for advice, White Cloud told
Black Hawk that a great Indian confederacy of tribes would
come to the Sauks' rescue if the Americans attacked. He also
predicted that the British would send men, arms, and ammunition via the Great Lakes to help the villagers. No one had promised any of these things, but because the Indians respected
White Cloud's status as a shaman, his predictions got serious
consideration.

Thus, when the British Band and other adherents accepted
Black Hawk's call to return to Saukenuk during the spring of
1832, the group lacked firm, experienced leadership. Instead,
rash and blustering young Napope, White Cloud, who was in
good standing with neither the Sauk nor the Winnebago tribal
leaders, and Black Hawk, now some sixty-five years old and not
an experienced civil leader, combined to direct the affairs of the
British Band. By the summer the group had little coherence,
but had a recognized leadership structure of its own: this consisted of nine chiefs, including White Cloud; Napope;
Weesheet, another thirty-five year old man; and six others. In
addition, the band recognized five war captains including:

Black Hawk, "the leader of all"; Kinnekonnesaut; Menacou; Makatauauquat; and Pashetowat. Of the nine recognized chiefs, only four had signed the June 30, 1831 agreement with General Gaines, while among the war captains only Black Hawk and Menacou had then been recognized leaders. By the time the British Band recrossed the Mississippi River in April of 1832, it had taken on at least the organizational identity of a separate tribal group. Nevertheless, when the disastrous war ended that August, Quashquame and White Cloud both said that the chiefs were all too young to lead a village.

Many factors motivated these men and their followers throughout the fateful 1831–32 events. Fundamental to an understanding of the Indians' actions in 1832 is the fact that the so-called British Band lacked any basic coherence. Not an identified part of either the Sauk or Mesquakie tribes, it combined disaffected elements from both. It also included as many as one hundred Kickapoo warriors and their families who had belonged to a village that had split from their rest of the tribe in 1819 and had established a separate community at the mouth of the Rock River where they remained closely associated with the people of Saukenuk. The Kickapoos contributed no principal leaders to the British Band, and most of their warriors died during the war. White Cloud's village also joined the British Band, bringing another one hundred or so people to it. These groups merged with a solid core from Saukenuk. In fact the Sauks and the Mesquakie people comprised the bulk of the group. They included perhaps four hundred warriors or men and older boys, with the women and other children probably doubling the total. Another fifty or so from the Mesquakie village at Dubuque fled to Black Hawk's group to escape punishment for the 1831 killings of the Menominees at Prairie du Chien. Clearly the British Band included a wide assortment of people who had little in common other than anger at the whites and resentment aimed at their own tribal leaders.

Those Mesquakies fleeing white demands for justice had a readily understandable reason for joining the British Band.

Certainly in their own eyes, as well as those of other Indians of
the region, they had ample justification for their 1831 attack on
the Menominees. That tribe and the Sioux had killed their
chiefs while the latter tried to make peace as ordered by the government. As a result they considered the deaths murder and not
simply acts of warfare. As such, tribal custom demanded retaliation. When the Mesquakies did this successfully, the American
authorities demanded that tribal leaders surrender those responsible for the killing. The outraged Mesquakies fled to Black
Hawk's camp, where they asked the old warrior for his advice.
He reported telling them that their conduct was correct and that
"our Great Father acted very unjustly, in demanding [their sur-
render] when he had suffered all their chiefs to be decoyed away,
and murdered by the Menominees...."

The fugitive group and the Kickapoos seemed to have had little to lose by joining the British Band, but the motivations for
most of the eight hundred or so Sauks and Mesquakies who followed Black Hawk's lead were more complex. The incidents between settlers and villagers at Saukenuk the preceding two or
three summers had caused much personal animosity. The fool-
hardy pioneers had beaten and even killed Indian men, insulted
and beaten the women, and in general had angered the Sauks.
The memories of these events, coupled with a perceived sexual
threat that white men posed to the Indian women, frightened
and outraged the Sauks. During the winter of 1831–32 rumors of
American plans to destroy the Indians circulated widely in the
hunting camps. In fact, these stories spread throughout the
camps so that even the peaceably inclined civil chiefs of both the
Sauk and Mesquakie tribes reported them to officials. According to the rumors, which the chiefs labeled "fables," the whites
planned to take all of the Indian males and "deprive them of
those parts which are said to be essential to courage...." Then
the Americans would bring "a horde of Negro men" to breed
with the Sauk women to produce a new stock of slaves and at the
same time obliterate the Saukenuk people.

The cooperative chiefs sought to make the whites aware of the impact that this and other stories had on the thinking of many British Band members. They noted that the women had urged their husbands to take part in the move back into Illinois with an "enthusiastic madness," perhaps proving that they feared that the stories were true. Black Hawk himself admitted that the women had strongly supported him in the decision to move east across the Mississippi, but he made no allusion to rumors of castration of the men and forced sexual unions with blacks for the women. Later the peaceful leaders also noted that during the fighting in 1832 the dissident warriors "uniformly treated the dead bodies of the unfortunate white men who had fallen into their hands, with the same indignities which they themselves so much dreaded." Whether these fears actually served to persuade disaffected individuals and small groups to join the British Band or were a later rationalization remains unclear. The fact that responsible tribal leaders reported at the time that such ideas circulated widely throughout the winter camps of both tribes certainly indicates the degree of paranoia and fear then existing among the Indians.

While some of the Sauks and Mesquakies feared future American actions against them, many resented the results of past dealings with the whites. Continuing efforts by the frontier Indian officials to keep the different tribes apart and at peace proved offensive to the Indians. They felt that the whites were meddling in intertribal affairs—an area where the Indians had long-accepted practices of diplomacy of their own. When the government stepped between contending tribes and took over the responsibility of covering the blood for Indian deaths and injuries, the action struck at the heart of tribal independence and self-esteem. The warriors could not be true to their culture, their clan, or families if they could not retaliate against their real or perceived enemies: clearly that angered and frustrated many.

White improprieties extended far beyond interference in routine tribal diplomacy, however. By involving themselves in the

disputes between the Sauks and Mesquakies and their Sioux enemies, the Americans also played a major role in disrupting the
tribal economies. The whites failed to protect tribal hunting
grounds from either Indian enemies or from encroachment by
pioneers and thus disrupted Indian hunting and trapping, jeop-
ardized their relationships with private traders, and brought the
threat of starvation to the villagers. As the chief providers of
food and claimants to the land around Saukenuk, the women
hated the whites for taking their well-prepared fields. So the
women supported the return to Illinois because they thought
that the whites had robbed them of their land and destroyed
their rightful place within the tribal economy. Long-time complaints such as continual white incursions on lead lands had
brought only limited relief from the government. The fact that
the Illinois militiamen had dug up the ancestral graves when
they destroyed Saukenuk in June 1831 also infuriated many
within the British Band. Looking at the situation that year, few
Indians could do more than mourn or rage at their oppressors.
They had real and long-standing grievances. All that remained
was for someone or something to ignite and channel the rage
lurking near the surface of many psyches during the 1831–32
winter.

Several related events galvanized the semiretired Black Hawk
into renewed leadership. During that same winter, White Cloud
twice sent messages to the Sauk hunting camps inviting the British Band to "join him at his village, there to live." This invitation was of major importance in explaining the actions British
Band leaders took in 1832. The invitation had rekindled Black
Hawk's hopes of spending his last years along the Rock River,
even if some miles upstream from his beloved Saukenuk. The
prophet made no secret of his invitations, even telling agent St.
Vrain about them that spring. The news caught the agent completely off guard. By this time he had assumed that the use
of troops in 1831, to drive the Indians west, had settled the issue. When St. Vrain explained the situation, the prophet insisted that he knew nothing of the June 1831 agreement that prohibited the Indians from recrossing the Mississippi.

Had White Cloud merely invited the British Band to settle near his village, nothing might have happened. However, he extended the offer after Napope brought stirring news from his visit to Fort Malden late the preceding summer. Once again, he claimed that the British had told him that if the tribe had not sold its land to the government, the Americans could not take it away from them. Black Hawk had heard that before, but this time Napope had new information. He reported that if the government tried to force the tribe off its land and a war resulted, the British would help the Indians! This was almost too good to be true, but Napope had other dramatic things to tell his eager listeners as well.

Not only had the young chief discussed these matters with the British, but he had also stopped at the prophet's village on his return. White Cloud told Napope that he had received messages from the British promising guns, ammunition, provisions, and clothing the next spring. Ships would bring these things to Milwaukee from Canada. White Cloud also said that he had gotten wampum and tobacco from several of the other Great Lakes area tribes including the Ottawas, Ojibwas, Potawatomis, and Winnebagoes. According to the enthusiastic messenger, the prophet had promised that each of those tribes would fight alongside the British Band if it became necessary and that the British would support all of them. If somehow the Indians failed and the Americans defeated them, White Cloud said that safety lay to the north, having received a friendly message from the leaders of the Selkirk colony on the Red River of the North inviting the Indians to Canada.

Black Hawk had no way to know that the entire story was nothing more than a string of lies. His political inexperience led him to accept what Napope had told him. The chief had said what Black Hawk yearned to hear and covered his words with the authority of the prophet, whose advice the old warrior respected, so Black Hawk failed to ask any pointed questions. Napope told him that they both needed to visit White Cloud's village, but that Black Hawk should stay in Iowa until he made up his mind about what course of action to take. Two years later

Black Hawk

the old warrior recalled the incident happily. After considering Napope's news carefully, he noted that he "was pleased to think that, by a little exertion on my part, I could accomplish the object of all my wishes." The stories told by White Cloud and Napope overcame his good judgment by appealing to his wishful thinking. Having decided to follow their advice, he sent word to the prophet that he would gather the braves together for a council. There he would explain the good news Napope had delivered and recruit followers from all of the Sauk bands. Quickly he sent messengers to the major Sauk and Mesquakie camps, but Keokuk and the civil chiefs rejected his good news. Keokuk told him that he "had been imposed upon by liars" and that he had better remain where he was and keep quiet.

As soon as the Sauk chiefs learned of Black Hawk's proposal, Keokuk asked the agent and Clark at St. Louis for permission to lead a delegation to Washington to settle the difficulties. When he failed to win approval for that, the chief also asked George Davenport to see the president for the tribe while he was in Washington that winter. The trader did not get to see President Jackson, but Old Hickory would have had nothing more to say on the issue; he wanted the Indians west of the Mississippi and had no sympathy for their appeals. When the trader told the chiefs that nothing more could be done and the officials declined to lead them east, Black Hawk decided, the time had come to act. He blamed Keokuk and the civil chiefs for not standing up to the Americans in 1831 as the major cause of his having been forced west across the river. If the tribe had remained united and its leaders had acted bravely by refusing to vacate Saukenuk, the humiliating flight from the village during the night of June 25, 1831, would never have occurred. This time, he decided, the Sauks would not run from their enemies. With that in mind the aging warrior resumed recruiting followers for his final return to the banks of the Rock River.

Although it is impossible to know Black Hawk's motivations with certainty, his autobiography and later talks with public officials give a window through which to examine his thinking. Several reasons, rational and otherwise, for his actions seem apparent. Undoubtedly he chafed under the authority of the civil chiefs who had lost his respect by surrendering their Illinois lands without much protest. He disliked Keokuk in particular for his leadership skills and because he felt that the Watchful Fox had usurped his own rightful place as the principal war leader of the Sauk nation. Still, simple jealousy hardly seems enough to have persuaded him back into action. He had gotten a small cabin and plot of plowed land from the agent that autumn. His wife, sons, and daughter lived with him, and he even admitted to being ready to live in retirement. Clearly it took more than a slim chance to recapture past excitement or to relive previous military glory to convince him that he should lead an independent British Band back to Illinois.

For Black Hawk, being forced to flee his ancestral home during the night had proved to be the most humiliating experience of his life to that time. All of the Sauks who wanted to remain at Saukenuk resented the American force that had driven them west, but that helpless flight haunted the aging warrior during the months that followed. His self-image was that of a Sauk warrior, as his autobiography demonstrates vividly. He traced his ancestry back to Nanamakee, the earliest war chief in Sauk memory. That individual had received what Black Hawk described as "the great medicine bag," with the admonition that it is the "soul of our nation—it has never yet been disgraced—and I will expect you to keep it unsullied." That medicine bundle, he claimed, had passed through Nanamakee's descendants to his own father Pyesa, who gave it to him before he died. Having gotten the sacred bundle from his dying father, the young Sauk warrior thought of himself as bearing the responsibility to protect the tribe and to uphold Sauk military traditions and honor. To his fellow tribesmen, his detailed recounting of military exploits and brave actions was not boasting. Rather it was an expected and necessary part of retaining the tribal military heritage and of inspiring another generation of young Sauk men to follow the paths their elders had set before them.

At each new discussion of the 1804 treaty of cession, Black Hawk himself spoke against it or supported others who did. Black Hawk was convinced that Quashquame had not sold any land north of the Rock River and that, if the treaty included any such cession, the whites had put it in without telling the Sauks that it was there. He admitted signing the 1816 treaty, but again insisted that no discussion of having sold tribal lands along the Rock had taken place. His narrower objections and legalistic approach by the late 1820s seem to accept the 1804 cession, as he claimed the right to remain on unsold federal lands in Illinois. During the War of 1812 his determination to protect Sauk land claims led directly to his accepting the invitation to fight against the United States. Robert Dickson had gauged this feeling correctly and recruited him easily by assuring Black Hawk that the King's soldiers would keep Americans from taking any of the tribe's lands. While that effort and Black Hawk's later arguments about treaties all failed, in every instance his goal remained that of protecting Sauk rights and, in particular, their village and graves at Saukenuk.

As keeper of Sauk military tradition and reputation, Black Hawk frequently criticized Keokuk and the civil leaders as cowards because they chose negotiations and accommodation as the best means for dealing with the Americans. To the old warrior this smacked of incompetence or negligence. Black Hawk not only saw their actions as a failure to protect the tribe and its rights, but also, and at least as important, as the abandonment of Sauk military traditions. In fact, during the 1831–32 winter, while he considered the prophet's news of British and Indian help for the Sauks if they returned to Illinois, Black Hawk stressed the leaders' failure again. Indian expulsion from Saukenuk, he thought, was the direct result of the "peaceable disposition of Keokuk and his people." Had the civil chiefs offered more resistance to the Americans, Black Hawk felt certain that no troops would have been called to drive the Indians from their homes.

So looking to the medicine bundle as a reminder of Sauk hunting grounds, their rich, well-tended fields, and their home village, Black Hawk thought that Sauk culture must place a strong emphasis on following the dictates of earlier generations. In a society without monuments, public buildings, or written records or histories, the graves of ancestors represented the people's most tangible connection to the past. Not only had the whites driven the Sauks away and refused to allow them to return home, if only to visit the graves, but the militiamen had disturbed the bones of their deceased loved ones. In his anger over this desecration the old war leader served as a focal point for the discontentments of other villagers. The fact that the chiefs had failed to protect the graves from desecration both humiliated and outraged the Indians. They felt helpless, even debased, and looked for some means to regain their dignity.

Perhaps the principal factor in Black Hawk's decision to defy the American officials was his long-standing sense that they had continually dealt unfairly and dishonestly with the Sauks. The Treaty of 1804 was the beginning, for Black Hawk, of the American mistreatment. Later, on the eve of the War of 1812, the Americans disrupted the Sauk and Mesquakie trade with their long-established British partners. Then the Americans had lied about getting credit from the government trader so that the Indians would have enough food, clothing, and other supplies to survive their winter hunt. During the late 1820s and early 1830s when the people at Saukenuk had constant trouble with white squatters, their agent, the trader, and the commander at Fort Armstrong all refused to help; instead they said that they had no authority to order the pioneers to leave the Indian lands, even though a clause in the treaty guaranteed the Sauks the right to live on the land in question until the government had sold it. The attitude of superiority the squatters had displayed further infuriated Black Hawk. The squatters' complaints that the Indians were to blame for the difficulties were insufferable. "They made themselves out to be the injured party, and we the in-

truders!" he reported. "How smooth must be the language of
the whites, when they can make right look like wrong and
wrong look like right."

Finally, the way in which the Americans had intervened in the
dispute between the Mesquakies and the Menominees was the
last straw. Even Keokuk and the civil chiefs had agreed with
Black Hawk when he claimed that the Americans' actions were
a disgrace to his people.

Whether the old warrior thought through his reasons carefully or not is unimportant. He later reported that the decision
was an easy one and that he hoped that the people would be
happy again; if he could do something to accomplish that goal,
Black Hawk would be content. What emerges from the historical record is that disaffected Sauks, Mesquakies, Kickapoos,
and Winnebagoes all flocked to his standard quickly. During the
early spring of 1832 he sent runners to the hunting camps
throughout eastern Iowa calling on Sauks, Mesquakies, and
others to rendezvous near old Fort Madison on the Mississippi
River. In villages they controlled, the civil chiefs prohibited
Black Hawk's emissaries from recruiting whenever possible,
greatly reducing the magnetic attraction of their proposals. According to one unverified account, the recruiter who visited
Keokuk's own village proved most able and soon got an enthusiastic response. Stressing the many insults perpetrated against
the Indians by the whites, and promising rich booty, he soon
had the braves dancing around a war pole. The warriors called
on Keokuk to lead them, and he agreed. Then Keokuk cau-
tioned them that warfare against the long knives was hopeless,
but said that if they demanded that he do so he would lead them
despite the hopeless odds. Before doing that, however, he urged
them to kill all their wives and children to protect them from the
coming fury of the whites once the Sauks went to war. According to the story, that cooled the braves' enthusiasm and Black
Hawk's recruiter left the village emptyhanded.

Although a good story, it bears little resemblance to what occurred. Black Hawk certainly sent men to each of the other

hunting camps with invitations to join his group at Fort Madison. It is highly unlikely that they invited the rest of the Sauks and Mesquakies to join them in a frontier war against the whites, however. In fact, Black Hawk repeatedly urged his followers to avoid provocations. He had taken that approach in June 1831 when General Gaines arrived at Fort Armstrong with his regular army troops. Nevertheless, Black Hawk was aware that violence might occur, and stressed that the warriors remain alert to defend the rest of the people. Apparently he expected to avoid violence while traveling up the Rock River to the prophet's village. Here his reliance on White Cloud's dreams and promises shows him being hopelessly naive and grasping at straws. Why he thought that the whites would not attack his party when he had been forced to sneak away from the village during the night the year before to avoid bloodshed remains unclear. What is certain is that despite whatever some of the firebrands among his followers might have said, Black Hawk expected to remain at peace. If the whites left the British Band alone, its members would not begin hostilities. If the Americans disputed their passage near Fort Armstrong, the Indians would have to turn back. Once the Sauks reached the upper Rock River, however, the old leader expected reinforcements from the nearby tribes. He thought that with that help the British Band would be able "to withstand an army!"

While the Indians gathered near the Mississippi, the federal government was still focusing its attention on preventing possible retaliation of the Sioux and Menominees against the Mesquakies for their devastating raid of the previous summer. General Alexander Macomb, commanding general of the army, ordered General Atkinson to take the troops then at Jefferson Barracks and proceed north to Rock Island. From there he was to do everything in his power to prevent renewed intertribal hostilities. Atkinson got the orders on April 1 and immediately prepared his men for their journey. On April 8, 1832, the troops began their trip up the Mississippi aboard two steamboats. They reached Rock Island on April 12, and from there Atkinson sent messages to nearby tribal leaders, Indian agents, and military commanders. By then, however, it was already too late—not to stop a war between the Menominees and Sioux against the Sauks and Mesquakies, but rather to prevent Black Hawk from leading the British Band back into Illinois.

While the troops steamed up the Mississippi, Black Hawk had already begun his fateful march. With probably somewhat less than five hundred mounted warriors, the British Band now included hundreds of women, children, and old people. On April 6 the Indians had started their trek north from Fort Madison to Yellow Banks or present Oquawka, Illinois, where they crossed east over the Mississippi. Once on the Illinois side, the British Band sent the old people and children ahead with some one hundred pack horses and supplies. They were to hurry north to the prophet's village. The warriors and other adults proceeded by canoe and on horseback up the Mississippi to the Rock. Whites who saw the procession reported that the Indians were travelling "with flankers thrown out to reconnoiter, & are very strict and vigilant." This would have been in stringent accord with Sauk travel customs for passing through a dangerous region.

As the band neared the mouth of the Rock and then turned northeast up that stream, Indian scouts reported that General Atkinson had reached Fort Armstrong with several hundred more troops. Black Hawk worried that Atkinson might use the two steamboats to blockade the mouth of the Rock, or that the general had stationed his troops along the low bluffs and in the ravines to attack the Indians as they moved through the area. To keep up the spirits of his party, he ordered the warriors to beat their drums and to sing their war songs. He hoped that this would also prove to the Americans that the Sauks did not fear them. To his relief no sudden volleys tore into the Indian ranks as they passed up the mouth of the Rock slowly and without incident.

By this time the British Band included the Sauk and Mesquakie warriors who had gathered at Fort Madison, plus another one hundred Kickapoo men and the Sauks and

Winnebagoes from White Cloud's village. All totaled their numbers might have reached six hundred fighting men, but it is likely that the number remained slightly less than that. When the dependents are added to that figure, the group may have numbered somewhere near two thousand people. Had the Indians been able to settle unopposed at the prophet's village, some forty miles up the Rock River, they might have been able to sustain themselves that summer. Because war broke out only some six weeks after they recrossed the Mississippi, however, they never had a chance to plant any crops, and by late that summer they faced starvation.

All that lay in the future, however, as the Indians, relieved that the soldiers had allowed them to pass up the Rock, halted only six or eight miles upstream from Fort Armstrong. Even though the British Band was so close, Atkinson did nothing to hinder their travel further up the Rock. Instead, on April 13, he called the friendly Sauk and Mesquakie chiefs to a council at the Fort. Still trying to carry out his previous orders, he hoped to get the tribal leaders to surrender the men responsible for the attack on the Menominees the previous summer. This effort failed. The friendly chiefs told Atkinson that they had no control over the people he sought. Possibly half of them had joined Black Hawk's group, and the rest were in Iowa hunting. The civil chiefs assured the general that they would stay away from the British Band, but flatly refused to try to get the murderers or to surrender hostages in their stead. Thus the council did little except to give the dissident Sauks and their companions more time to move up the Rock River.

While Atkinson talked with the peaceful leaders, he also sought to gain information about the movements of the British Band and its intentions. He hurried up the Mississippi to review the troops at Prairie du Chien and left orders there for the coming weeks. Then he returned to Fort Armstrong. In the meantime Black Hawk and his followers had arrived at the prophet's village. On April 16, Atkinson sent Appenoose, a Mesquakie warrior, and a companion to the dissidents' camp. The members of the British Band assumed that the two men were spies and treated them roughly. They threatened them, boasted about how many warriors from the Kickapoo, Potawatomi, and Winnebago tribes had joined them, threatened to make war against the whites, and shouted down any suggestion that the group move back across the Mississippi. Their boasts, if heard by any whites, would have caused panic in the frontier settlements, but it is unlikely that the civilian population ever did hear them. Nevertheless, boasts were not what the general had expected. His orders were to prevent a war between contending tribes of Indians, not to engage in one against them.

On April 24, Atkinson sent two young Sauk leaders to deliver a message to Black Hawk. "Your great father will be angry with you for" recrossing the Mississippi, he wrote. After encouraging the Indians to return to Iowa quickly, he advised that it was "not too late to do what is right" and concluded, "if your hearts are good I will send an officer to talk with you in three or four days." Black Hawk apparently considered the message a threatening order that the British Band retrace its steps down the Rock and then back across the Mississippi; he rejected it. The White Beaver, as the Indians called Atkinson, had no right to make such a demand. All the group intended to do was to travel to the prophet's village where they expected to settle down and plant their summer crops. Again, Black Hawk claimed that as long as he and the others remained peaceable, the whites would have no cause to disturb them.

The old warrior tried to shift responsibility for the actions of the British Band to its young chiefs and to absolve himself from any blame for their move into Illinois. In the answer he sent to Atkinson he asked why the whites had bothered to ask him his motivations. After denying that he commanded the Indians, Black Hawk said that he merely followed the chiefs who led the village. "I have no bad feelings" toward the whites, he said. Clearly, fundamental differences on how they should respond to the whites' demands that they leave the Rock River area divided the Indian camp. Black Hawk knew enough to at least claim peaceful intentions at this point, while some of the others in the group differed about that. Napope, speaking for the British Band leaders, responded negatively to the White Beaver's demands: he refused to go back to Iowa. "I had no bad intention when I came up the Rock River," he said, "I was invited by the Winnebagoes" and expect to live with them. Yet this was not to be.

While the two Sauk emissaries visited the camp, Henry Gratiot, the Winnebago subagent, and some of the Winnebago leaders arrived at the prophet's village. Accompanied by another white man; Whirling Thunder; White Crow, the Winnebago leader often called The Blind because he had lost an eye and wore a cloth over that side of his face; and another twenty-four Winnebago warriors, Gratiot reached the British Band encampment at a crucial time. The two Mesquakies were about to leave with the news that the Indian leaders insisted that they would continue farther up the Rock River. The agent had to depend upon White Crow to be the interpreter, and this proved unfortunate. Gratiot urged his listeners to give up their idea of settling in northern Illinois and to return peacefully to Iowa. He had General Atkinson's letter read and tried to explain it carefully to the Indians, but with little success. What he failed to realize was that his interpreter told him one thing while the British Band leaders had said another. It is uncertain what his motives were, but instead of merely relating the agent's views, the troublesome Winnebago urged the Sauks to continue up the Rock and promised that hundreds of Winnebago warriors would help them if the whites challenged their movement.

That night and much of the next day the Indians held war dances and raised a British flag at the council site. The leaders told the warriors that the White Beaver had threatened to pursue them and to force them back across the Mississippi. That and the urgings of White Cloud kindled a hostile spirit in the camp, and at one point Gratiot and his white companion wondered whether they would be allowed to leave. Indian ceremonial custom demanded that guests not be made prisoners or harmed in any way, however, and so a day after the two young

Sauk messengers had returned to Atkinson, the agent and his companion, accompanied by several of the Winnebagoes, left as well; they traveled quickly to Fort Armstrong where they reported to Atkinson immediately.

The meeting with Gratiot and the Winnebago leaders proved to be the high point for the British Band. The Indians thought that they had plenty of support from nearby tribes and that American forces would not attack them as long as they remained at peace. At the same time many of the less-disciplined warriors had taken some of the harsh rhetoric their leaders used to heart. They performed their war dance for hours, sharpened their weapons, and bragged of using the lances they had killed the Menominees with a year earlier against any whites foolish enough to come after them. At this point, apparently, Black Hawk still believed that the Sauks could remain with the Winnebagoes. In fact, he returned General Atkinson's letter with Gratiot, with the message that he intended to remain on the Rock River. He did say that the Indians would not start any hostilities, but that they certainly would defend themselves if attacked.

This period of euphoria soon ended, however, as the Indian leaders realized the gravity of their situation. Having decided that the White Beaver would come after them soon, the chiefs began seeking allies and support. They had only a modest amount of corn and other food and would need the entire summer to raise new crops, so it became imperative that they choose a village site quickly. To Black Hawk's chagrin, the leaders of the Winnebago villages did not welcome the dissidents with much enthusiasm. In fact, the tribe had decidedly mixed feelings about the British Band and its movement toward their territory. Earlier, some tribesmen had responded favorably to the wampum and bundles of tobacco dyed red, but those at the prophet's village told the dissidents to stay there that season. While admitting that they had sent wampum calling for an alliance during the preceding winter, the Winnebagoes now said that they had changed their minds. If the whites had no objections, they said, the British Band might stay with the prophet and raise their crops at his village. That was a far cry from the stories that Napope and White Cloud had told Black Hawk. Not only did the Winnebagoes refuse to join the dissidents as full allies, but even worse, they would not give the hungry Sauks and Mesquakies food, much less welcome them into their tribal territory.

At this point Black Hawk began to suspect that Napope and White Cloud had lied when they described how much help the British Band might expect from their neighbors. That night he accused Napope of misleading them, but asked the chiefs to keep the news from the rest of the band until they met with the Potawatomis in a few days. Perhaps only the Winnebagoes would prove to be false allies. So after Black Hawk and the other leaders told the people that they expected help from the British at Milwaukee in just a few days, the group set out north and east once more. At the Kishwacokee River, near present Rockford, Illinois, the Sauks sent messengers to the Potawatomi villages asking the chiefs for a council. When the delegates arrived, Black Hawk asked if they had much extra corn at their villages. To his dismay, they said that they had no surplus and could spare little if any. After receiving several more "unsatisfactory answers," Black Hawk asked the Potawatomi representatives to meet secretly with the leaders that evening. Unhappily they reported hearing nothing from the British at Milwaukee or elsewhere, and that they knew nothing of promises of military aid to the Sauks.

Black Hawk sent the messengers back to their villages with the request that their chiefs come to talk as soon as possible. At that point he decided "that if the White Beaver came after us, we would go back—as it is useless to think of stopping or going on without provisions." The next day the Potawatomi chiefs arrived, and British Band leaders prepared a dog feast for the visitors. During the meal Black Hawk laid out the tribal medicine bundle he had cared for since his teens. Whether he hoped that the power of the charm might influence the Potawatomis' decisions concerning his group is unclear, and he said no more about it. Before the feast ended, a messenger arrived and told the chiefs that several hundred mounted white men had been seen less than ten miles away. At this the Potawatomis left hurriedly, and Black Hawk sent three warriors with a white flag to arrange a council with the whites. He wanted to negotiate a safe passage back down the Rock to the Mississippi so that his followers might return safely to Iowa.

That never happened, however, because the approaching whites proved to be Illinois militiamen and not regular army troops. When Black Hawk had sent the braves to the whites' camp, it never occurred to him that no interpreter would be present. The excited militiamen surrounded the three young Indians and hurried them into camp. There, several of the whites saw other Indians, who were trying to learn something, watching from a nearby ridge. Suspecting Indian treachery, the whites seized the three with the white flag and set out full tilt to capture the rest, firing as they rode. The whites killed several of Black Hawk's scouts, and the survivors raced back to camp to warn the chiefs of the whites' treachery. Now there seemed to be little choice. Black Hawk had tried to settle the impasse peacefully, only to have his scouts attacked and one of his emissaries killed. He ordered the several dozen warriors then still in camp to form a skirmish line behind some low shrubs and waited for the whites to attack. They did, but in such a thoroughly disorganized rush that the Indians terrified them with a well-timed volley and drove them across the prairie in panic. Only a modest number of fatalities occurred at Stillman's Run, the scene of the battle, but it was enough to set into motion a conflict that destroyed the British Band.

Thus, what began as a yearning to return peaceably to their homeland, an effort to demonstrate Sauk honor, anger at being treated so cavalierly by the pioneers and the government, and simple misinformed wishful thinking turned into an unexpected war. Black Hawk had claimed repeatedly that he expected to live among the Winnebagoes and that he would fight only if at-

tacked, although from time to time he said and did things that
seemed to contradict that. Whatever the excitable young warriors thought, as a seasoned veteran of many campaigns, Black
Hawk knew that the British Band lacked enough food to feed itself for more than just a few weeks. By the time the Illinois militia attacked his camp, he had accepted the fact that neither the
other tribes nor the British would offer any help. Napope and
the prophet had lied to him, and now he had to get his group to
Iowa safely. Had General Atkinson restrained the mounted militiamen and sent regular troops with an effective interpreter to
the scene, the war could have been avoided easily. As the aging
Sauk later said, "my object was not war. I sent a flag of peace to
the American war chief." When the whites attacked, "I was
forced into war...."

The Battle of Stillman's Run had a number of unfortunate
results. In the short term, it provided the Indians badly needed
food, blankets, and other camp equipment and ammunition left
by the fleeing whites. The victory may well have persuaded the
British Band that they could fight their way back to the Mississippi because the frontiersmen had been such cowards. The militiamen's behavior certainly mystified Black Hawk. He
commented that generally Americans fought and shot well.
"Never was I so much surprised in my life, as I was in this attack," he recalled. The white army of three or four hundred
men had started shooting after they learned that he was asking
for peace. Breaking all precedent, at least in his experience in
dealing with other Indians, with the British, and with Americans in the War of 1812 era, they had tried to kill his unarmed
flag bearers. Even more astounding, when they attacked with
ten times as many men as he had, his small line of skirmishers
so terrified them that they fled. He had expected to see the militiamen fight as well as the American troops he had faced during
the War of 1812, "but they had no such braves among them."

Despite his momentary astonishment at the troops' behavior,
Black Hawk already realized that his entire venture had been a
mistake. He had only five hundred warriors and knew that the

whites could raise many times that number. He feared that if the
British Band tried to return down the Rock they would be destroyed, so he now sought a safe place for the women and children. Having sent scouts to track the Americans' movements,
he renewed the band's ascent up the Rock. On the way a party
of Winnebago warriors came to the camp as volunteers to fight
against the whites. These men carried out several raids during
the next few weeks, killing the Sauk agent St. Vrain and four
other men in that area. While the war parties moved across
northern Illinois, the rest of the British Band made its way
slowly toward the four lakes at present Madison, Wisconsin.

Having been forced into war by the actions of Stillman's militia force, Black Hawk now turned to directing that effort with
care. He called in the scouts and the small war parties and began to plan the Indians' actions. To inspire the warriors he held
another dog feast. Again he took out the sacred medicine bundle. Reminding his listeners that the bundle had been handed
down from Mukataquet, "the father of the Sauk nation," he
told them that their ancestors had never disgraced the medicine
bag. As he concluded he said that he expected each of the men
to protect the sacred tribal symbol. Then they turned to the
feast. Throughout the war months the old warrior used tradition
and ceremony repeatedly to inspire and tie the disparate group
together. Apparently his efforts succeeded, and although con-
temporaries tended to describe him as inarticulate, or at least in-
effective as a public debater with Keokuk, his inspirational talks
were successful.

While the Indians launched a growing number of raids
against the frontier settlements, their victory at Stillman's Run
began to invite wholesale disaster for them later that summer.
The terrified volunteers had fled the scene of their defeat
spreading news of the debacle, and with every telling of their
battle stories the size of the Indian force grew. General Atkinson
and his regular army officers could only shake their heads in dis-
belief and anger. Colonel Taylor, a 1814 victim of Black Hawk's
martial skills, later described the militia defeat with contempt.

Instead of fighting and defeating their enemy, he wrote "they became panic struck & fled in the most shameful manner...."

For Atkinson the news brought more than simple indignation; it signified the failure of his careful moves to prevent a frontier conflict. He had organized his forces on May 8, 1832, when he mustered some 1,700 Illinois militiamen into federal service and combined them with the 340 regular army troops then under his command. Then he ascended the Rock with the regular infantry while sending the mounted militiamen ahead to find the British Band. Perhaps he hoped that the mounted troops would locate and destroy the Indian fighting force. Perhaps he wanted to distance himself from that motley hoard of frontiersmen masquerading as soldiers. Whatever his reasoning, the move had brought Stillman's men into their disastrous contact with the Indians. When the general learned of the defeat, he complained that the ease of the Indian victory "not only encouraged the Indians but closed the door against settling the difficulty without bloodshed."

Early reports of Stillman's disaster claimed at least fifty-two whites killed and others wounded or captured. By the time the troops got organized enough to take an accurate count, they found that the militia had suffered only eleven fatalities and a few more casualties. Despite that, reports of the higher figures reached Washington long before any accurate count did and called forth angry demands that the army punish the British Band before allowing it to surrender. Even before the hostilities began, President Jackson had ordered that unless the Indians surrendered Black Hawk and other leaders to be kept as hostages for the good behavior of the Indians, General Atkinson was to "attack and disperse them...." This order left the general with little choice of action even prior to Stillman's Run. After the defeat, pioneers, frontier politicians, and federal officials alike clamored for retribution, the sooner the better.

By May 26, Atkinson had led the infantry south to Dixon's Ferry on the Rock River to resupply the troops, and Governor Reynolds had discharged a levy of Illinois militia. The governor then called for another two thousand troops to rendezvous in early June. While the army officers tried to supply their units and waited for the next batch of mounted volunteers to arrive and be put into something like military order, the Indians were carrying out a series of raids across the northern part of Illinois. On May 21, a forty-man war party of mostly Potawatomis struck one farming settlement, killing fifteen men, women, and children, and taking two young women, Sylvia and Rachel Hall, prisoners. They carried their prizes back to the main Sauk camp where the terrified sisters remained for the next nine days. Eventually the Sauks turned the girls over to some Winnebagoes, who delivered them to the whites in early June.

The entire incident, called the Indian Creek Massacre, demonstrates the variety of Indian motivations during the war and the difficulty of determining just which group bore the responsibility for specific actions. In this case the attack resulted from an incident in which a local farmer had whipped one of the Potawatomis severely, and the Indian used the unsettled conditions during the war to enlist his friends and relatives to gain revenge. A young Indian had warned the settlers that a war party was on its way to kill them, but apparently the whites failed to heed the warning. Black Hawk claimed that two young Sauk warriors who had accompanied the war party saved the young women, put them on their own horses and brought them back to the main camp before the other warriors could kill them. While that may have been just an after-the-fact effort to reduce criticism of his people, the Hall sisters did report that they had received good treatment while at the Indian camp.

The biggest problem the leaders of the British Band faced during much of the 1832 summer was to find enough food to keep their people from starvation. So while the whites struggled to get their military forces in order and to stockpile supplies and ammunition for the troops, the raids on frontier settlements continued. To accomplish this and to focus the enthusiasm of the warriors, Black Hawk led a two-hundred-man war party west toward the mining center of Galena. On June 24 the Sauks

and Mesquakies attacked a small stockaded fort on Apple
Creek, approximately fifteen miles southeast of Galena. The
small garrison housed only twenty-five men along with some
women and children who had taken refuge there. The Indians
shot one man outside the fort, but the pioneers managed to
close the gates, so the warriors settled down to shoot at anyone
who tried to look over the stockade. After an entire day of waiting and being able to fire only sporadically at anyone, Black
Hawk decided that the war party could do the most good by
gathering food and other supplies, so they broke into several of
the nearby cabins. From them they took flour and other food as
well as horses and some of the other livestock that had been left
untended in the fields when the settlers had fled to the fort.
Then the war party headed east with their booty.

As they rode away from their attack on the little fort, some of
the defenders, now reinforced, came after the raiders. The
Sauks hid in the woods, and then, with their rifles blazing, the
yelling warriors attacked their pursuers. For a time the pioneers
retreated, but soon they advanced with even more men. Major
John Dement, who led the whites, drew the Sauk leader's praise
for his courage and leadership. Although most of his men retreated, the Major and a few others fought bravely, inflicting
critical casualties on the Indians. In fact, two of the chiefs and
several others died in this battle. When the whites had retreated,
the warriors continued their journey back to the main camp,
with the food and livestock they had secured. Black Hawk must
have breathed a sigh of relief that the pioneers did not follow any
farther, because the whites had fought so well. "The young
[white] chief deserves great praise for his courage and bravery,"
the old warrior reported, "but, fortunately for us, his army was
not all composed of such brave men."

In the long run, when the leaders of the British Band had chosen to spend their time leading or directing raids against the
frontier settlements instead of hurrying north and west to the
Mississippi, they had brought disaster to their followers. Gradually, General Atkinson got his disorganized forces into motion,

and by June he had mounted militia units operating out of Galena under Colonel Henry Dodge, an effective frontier leader. As the regular troops moved north from Dixon's Ferry, the General had assembled a militia army of three regiments, as well as Potawatomi, Winnebago, Sioux, Menominee, and Stockbridge Indian auxiliaries to help him locate and defeat the dissident band. On July 3, scouts rode into camp with exciting news. They had found the trail of their quarry near Lake Koshkonong, a large marsh up the Rock River in southern Wisconsin. With that news, Atkinson halted his columns and sent more mounted men on ahead to scour the country for the elusive Sauks.

The British Band, meanwhile, had broken into small components and scattered as the nearly starved Indians hunted desperately for food. Apparently some went east toward Lake Michigan while the rest drifted slowly northward. As they lived for some weeks in the Four Lakes area, they found that it offered little food. Black Hawk complained that although the region provided safety from pursuit because of its marshy nature, the hunters found little game and the waters of the streams had few fish. Because their camp lay so far from other Indian villages or any white settlements, the British Band had nowhere to go for supplies either. Malnutrition weakened all of the Indians and some actual starvation occurred among the elderly and others who were sickly before the summer journey had begun. "We were forced to dig roots and bark trees, to obtain something to satisfy hunger and keep us alive," Black Hawk reported. At that point he decided that the only hope for survival was to move the women and children west across the Mississippi to the relative safety of their Sauk and Mesquakie relatives. Little did he realize that American officials had recruited large numbers of Sioux and Menominee warriors just in case he tried this tactic. Those men would attack and kill or capture most of the women and children who actually managed to get back across the Mississippi.

His decision to move the British Band west to the big river led to their discovery by the whites. By this time the national authorities from President Jackson down had joined in a chorus of denunciation of General Atkinson's conduct of the hunt for the Indians. It seemed to the officials that all Atkinson had done was to complain about a shortage of supplies while war parties crisscrossed the frontier raiding almost at will. The president became so angry when the army could not even find its foes, much less defeat them, that he dispatched General Winfield Scott with another several hundred regular army troops to take command. As this body of men traveled west via the Great Lakes, the troops contracted cholera, which was sweeping the country that summer, so they never got into action. Just the realization that he was about to be relieved for having failed to carry out the campaign angered Atkinson, and he struggled after the retreating Indians.

Still, the beleaguered general had too little food for his men, so on July 9 he dispatched several units north to Fort Winnebago on the Wisconsin River. When the militia got there they were tired, hungry, and angry at having failed to find the Indians. Fearing that the troops would abandon the campaign unless they took some strong action, the commanders, Colonel Dodge and Generals Milton Alexander and James Henry, decided that some of them should follow new leads brought in by some local Winnebago men. Alexander chose to obey Atkinson's orders and return to the main camp, while the other two set out to the northeast, anticipating that they would catch their foes at last. To their chagrin they found only a small Winnebago village and no clear signs indicating where the British Band might have gone. On July 19, 1832, the disappointed officers sent several messengers to tell General Atkinson the bad news, and on their way south to the main camp these men located the trail of the retreating British Band.

This discovery brought the frustrating summer campaign to an end almost as quickly as it had begun. While the messengers hurried to Atkinson's camp with their electrifying news, Dodge and Henry set out after the retreating Sauks. The thought that they might actually overtake the Indians spurred the tired men to greater effort as they rode across the countryside. For the next several days they encountered growing evidence of the Indians' passage: abandoned pots, blankets, and other camp equipage littered the trail. Then the pursuers began to encounter small groups of warriors who tried to slow their progress, and frequently the white leaders had to put their forces into skirmish lines. Bodies of elderly people and children lined the route of march too, as the starving Indians staggered on just ahead of the militiamen.

Late on the afternoon of July 21, the militia force overtook the exhausted Indians. In a steady rain the men under Dodge and Henry attacked the Sauk rear guard as the warriors sought to keep the whites from discovering that the main body of Indians was even then crossing the Wisconsin River. Napope led a small force of twenty warriors in a futile effort to halt the whites' advance. Black Hawk then coordinated the river crossing and defense with about fifty other men. The charging militiamen drove the Sauk defenders from a small hill and down into a nearby ravine from where the Indians continued to pour a heavy fire into the advancing ranks of the whites. At about 7 o'clock in the evening, with the light almost gone, Dodge and Henry decided to halt the attack. They would have had to cross an open river bottom into the fire of well-hidden warriors in poor light, and they understandably had little enthusiasm for such a tactic. In addition, their men had traveled on inadequate food or rest for the past several days and needed to rest almost as badly as did their foes.

So as darkness descended on the scene, the last of the Sauk rear guard slipped across the river and the whites went into camp, tired, but excited at having located the British Band at last. Not only had the militiamen found the Indians, but they gave the British Band a bad mauling too. In his account of the battle, Dodge reported that his Winnebago scouts had scalped eight of the dead while the whites scalped another thirteen men. In addition to those fatalities, he noted that the troops found eight more bodies the next morning and that three other warriors had died in skirmishing before the battle actually began. He estimated that "the numbers killed cannot fall short of forty," but admitted that there was no way to ascertain other Indian casualties because many of the wounded and perhaps even some of the dead had been carried away from the battle as the Sauks retreated. Black Hawk claimed to have lost only six men, but that may have only referred to the group of fifty warriors he used to cover the retreat and river crossing. One of the Sauk women later reported that as many as sixty-eight Indians died in the battle or while crossing the Wisconsin River.

Early in the predawn hours of July 22, Napope made an effort to end the conflict. Speaking in Winnebago, because he knew that Dodge's force had some guides from that tribe, he described the weakened condition of the women, children, and aged and called on the whites to allow the thoroughly demoralized Sauks to recross the Mississippi. Unfortunately for the Indians, those who understood Winnebago had left the militia camp. So instead of being allowed to surrender or to retreat without further attack, the chase continued. The Sauks had tried to communicate with their white pursuers at Stillman's Run and now again at Wisconsin Heights. In both cases the lack of an effective interpreter among the militia hindered the Indians' efforts to surrender and brought increased death and destruction. After making his futile plea to the militia, Napope and a companion fled to a nearby Winnebago village where they remained for the rest of the war. This defection angered Black Hawk and several of the other leaders because they blamed the young chief's lies about British and Indian support for having gotten them into their desperate straits in the first place.

Napope was not the only person to leave, as the Battle of Wisconsin Heights broke much of the remaining cohesion of the British Band. Earlier, groups of Winnebagoes and Potawatomis had joined the Sauks and Mesquakies, but even before this incident they had faded back into the countryside and returned to their own villages. For the retreating Indians, the hardship of their summer of constant movement, little food, and increasing danger had broken both their health and morale. They wanted no more fighting. One large group of mostly Mesquakie women and children used hastily made canoes to descend the Wisconsin River, hoping to slip south of the troops and return to their relatives in Iowa. This tactic failed. Roving bands of Winnebago and Menominee warriors captured many of the fugitives. Captain Gustavus Loomis, then commanding the regular troops at Fort Crawford at Prairie du Chien, asked the Indian agent there to have the Winnebagoes visit the Mesquakies with a flag of truce to get them to surrender peacefully. Despite this effort to prevent the wholesale slaughter of noncombatants, many women and children died. A guard of soldiers at the ferry some five miles from the mouth of the Wisconsin fired at numerous canoes as the panicked Indians tried to sneak past them. Some people in the canoes died of gunshot wounds or drowned trying to escape. Black Hawk claimed that many of those who did get past the soldiers starved to death in the woods.

While the Sauks headed northwest from the Wisconsin toward the Mississippi, General Atkinson rushed the rest of his force after them, meeting with the militia units under Dodge and Henry. On July 26, the general had reduced his little army to some 1300 and began crossing the men over the Wisconsin. Once over the river the race west began. True, the Indians had a five-day head start and probably had local Winnebago guides as well. The whites had never been in the region, but when they found the broad path left by the retreating Indians, the soldiers' morale soared. They realized the plight of the fugitives when they saw camp kettles, lodge mats, dead horses, and corpses of men wounded previously lying alongside the trail with those of children and elderly people who had died of malnutrition and starvation. The very fact that the Indians left no rear guard of warriors to harass or misdirect the rapidly gaining whites convinced Atkinson's men that they would soon overtake and destroy the last of Black Hawk's followers.

On August 1, 1832, the exhausted Indian survivors reached the banks of the Mississippi. Guided there by some of the Winnebagoes, they had expected to find canoes for the river crossing, but there were none. By this time the British Band numbered only about five hundred people because of battle deaths, starvation, or the continuing desertions of small groups during the preceding several weeks. The leaders halted for a council. They had few options: they could hurriedly build rafts and canoes and slip across the Mississippi; move north and break into small groups, hiding among the Winnebagoes; or they could wait for the arrival of the soldiers. Black Hawk recommended fleeing north to the Winnebago country, but few of his disheartened followers wanted anything more than a quick return to Iowa. So they hurriedly worked on canoes and rafts, and a few actually got across the Mississippi that day.

Most, however, never got that chance because the steamboat *Warrior* came into view. Black Hawk ordered the braves not to shoot at the boat and raised a white flag, hoping to be taken aboard the steamer to surrender. Once again, faulty translation foiled any chance to end the encounter peacefully. The interpreter on board the *Warrior* told the commanding officer that these Indians were Winnebagoes, not Sauks. Lieutenant James Kingsbury, commanding the boat and the troops aboard it, ordered that several of the Indians come aboard to clarify the situation, but the Indians on shore seem to have misunderstood his intentions and more confusion ensued. However it happened, instead of a parley and a peaceful surrender, the soldiers on the steamer opened fire on the unprepared Indians with their artillery piece and other weapons. After their initial surprise, the Sauks fought back, and late in the day the Warrior ran low on fuel so it returned to Prairie du Chien.

When the steamboat left, Black Hawk again called for a northward flight, this time to the Ojibwa villages, but by now he had almost no followers. Only four lodges, including White Cloud's, chose his alternative. During the night Black Hawk, White Cloud, and their small party left the main camp, traveling north to La Crosse. Most of the demoralized survivors wanted only to escape from the soldiers, and some swam across the Mississippi that same evening. The rest waited fearfully through the night, hoping to be able to get across the river the next morning before the nearby troops found them or the steamboat returned from Prairie du Chien.

On the evening of August 1, Atkinson's force stumbled into camp after dark. After a hurried supper, the exhausted men fell asleep, only to be jolted awake by a 2:00 a.m. bugle call. Gathering their equipment and weapons and collecting the horses, the troops started forward before dawn. After traveling a few miles, the advanced scouts met the rear guard of the Sauk camp. Henry Dodge's mounted troops killed some of the warriors and forced the rest into a slow retreat toward the Mississippi. The Indians tried every trick they knew to lure the whites away from the main camp, and for a time succeeded. Again, chance operated against the Sauks. The last of the militia regiments, than under Henry, found the trail to the Indian camp while most of the other troops moved off to the right, nearly missing their quarry. Atkinson's frustrated army fell on its foe with a vengeance. The modest number of warriors resisted stubbornly, trying to protect the women and children as the mothers struggled to get into the river with their little ones. Thoroughly outnumbered and heavily outgunned, the Sauk warriors had little chance. They retreated from one slough to another and then out onto the offshore islands in the river. Just then the *Warrior* reappeared, its artillery raking the small islands.

For eight hours the slaughter continued, with the soldiers lining the riverbanks firing at anything or anyone that moved. Fighting men, women, children, and the wounded received the same treatment. The soldiers shot at mothers swimming in the river with small children on their backs, and at times witnesses noted that blood flowed so freely that it tinted the water along the shores. Those who survived the attack from the steamer or the sharpshooters along the shore retreated into the water where the soldiers killed them. The number of Indians who actually died at this August 2 Battle of Bad Axe remains uncertain, in part because there is no accurate count of how many people remained at the British Band camp that day. Black Hawk had left with perhaps forty people the evening before the battle. Another hundred or so of the Sauks and Mesquakies had gotten across the Mississippi to safety, or so they thought. Unfortunately for them, the Sioux chief Wabashaw led a party of some 150 warriors after them at the behest of American officials. When the Sioux overtook the practically defenseless fugitives, they killed sixty-eight of them and took another twenty-two women and children prisoner. How many people that left to perish at Bad Axe is unclear, but estimates at the time suggest that at least 150 and perhaps as many as 300 of the British Band people died that grim morning. Atkinson's force had taken another thirty-nine women and children prisoner at the actual battle site. Of those, three died later.

The Battle of Bad Axe ended the sorry spectacle we now call the Black Hawk War. The Indians stumbled into these events because of lies, misinformation, and stubborn wishful thinking. The actual conflict began only because General Atkinson authorized the undisciplined and poorly led militia units to precede his regular army troops and to travel without an interpreter. Black Hawk had sent a small group to ask for peace talks with Stillman's militiamen only to have his men shot. During the night after the Battle at Wisconsin Heights, Napope tried to get the whites to agree to a surrender, but again the lack of an interpreter foiled that effort to end the fighting. Even their last-ditch white flag shown to troops aboard the *Warrior* brought a hail of lead instead of a chance to surrender. Perhaps as many as a thousand people may have died for nothing! Mistakes, incompetence, bitterness, and frontier hatreds combined to destroy the British Band. Black Hawk and some of the leaders survived, if only because they represented no further threat to the peace of the region. All of the destruction, misery, and death should have been avoided, but leaders, Indian and white alike, proved unwilling or unable to prevent this disastrous summer's conflict.

CHAPTER FIVE

Once I was a great warrior ♦ 1832–38

On July 4, 1838, Black Hawk rode into Fort Madison, Iowa, as an invited guest of the town fathers. By this time the citizens looked at the old warrior as a famous local character, so they asked him to attend their annual banquet. After they offered several toasts to "Our Illustrious Guest, Black Hawk," the townspeople called on him to speak. Two interpreters stood by. One translated his words to the crowd, the other recorded them, perhaps for an account of the festivities in the county newspaper. The aged Sauk thanked the whites for their friendship and food, and went on to recall fighting against them a few years earlier, even admitting doing wrong by fighting. But, he continued, he had loved his home and town and fought to save them. "I thank you for your friendship," he said. "Once I was a great warrior. I am now poor. . . . I am now old." This described Black Hawk's postwar status among the Sauks and the whites alike, as well as his own realization that his career as a leader had ended.

His descent from leadership took only about a year and began on the evening of August 1, 1832, when General Atkinson's little army had caught its breath before launching a devastating attack on the remnants of the British Band the next morning. That same evening Black Hawk, White Cloud, and perhaps another thirty or forty others left the main camp and began their trek north toward La Crosse. With his decision to abandon those who had followed him for the past six months, the aged warrior had given up any pretense to legitimate leadership within the Sauk tribe. Now he stood branded as an outcast from his own people and a fugitive from the whites.

What possessed him to flee in the face of danger rather than to stay to fight for personal and Sauk honor cannot be identified. According to his own account, all of Black Hawk's previous actions that year had resulted from his wish to help his followers. His effort to negotiate a safe passage back down the Rock River at Stillman's Run and his later use of a white flag when the *Warrior* appeared on August 1 both sought safety for the British Band. At the same time, his constant emphasis on Sauk tradition, honor, and personal bravery sounds hollow when contrasted to his flight the night prior to his followers' final crushing defeat.

Certainly by the night of August 1 Black Hawk realized that remaining to fight offered little hope of survival. It is even possible that he thought that if he and White Cloud both left the whites might be less inclined to punish their followers. Although personal survival certainly motivated him, Black Hawk may well have believed that he could blend into the countryside and remain hidden among the Winnebagoes. Throughout that fateful summer the Winnebago prophet and his followers had played an important role in the actions of the British Band. Others of that tribe had aided and encouraged the fugitives as well. White Crow had an instrumental role in persuading Black Hawk and the other Band leaders that they should proceed up the Rock River beyond the prophet's village at the beginning of the summer. In fact, later Indian testimony claimed that the Sauks and Mesquakies would have returned downriver had it not been for White Crow's promises of food, shelter, protection, and warriors for them. As well as fighting alongside the fugitives, Winnebago warriors guided the British Band from Lake Koshkonong west to the Wisconsin River and beyond that to the Mississippi. Women from that tribe exchanged corn, potatoes, and later canoes for mats, kettles, horses, and even ammunition and thus helped the refugees feed themselves during much of the summer. So the Winnebago region appeared as a logical place of refuge for Black Hawk and his companions.

Whatever his reasons for fleeing, the tired war leader moved northeast from the Bad Axe River toward the headwaters of the La Crosse River. There, just a short distance southwest of present Tomah, Wisconsin, his party rested for a few days. A passing Winnebago hunter found their camp without their knowing it and hurried downstream to inform the Winnebago leaders. At the village of Karayjasaip-ka or Winnebago Blackhawk, the hunter gave news of his discovery. Heated debate followed, but the chief persuaded his council that they should send messengers with a calumet to the fugitives. If they accepted and smoked the pipe, the Winnebagoes would ask the group to end the war, and under Indian custom the Sauks would have to agree. Five men set out for Black Hawk's camp, but three turned back. The last two, Chasja-ka or Wave, and Niroham-he-ke or He Who Illuminates the Water, continued their mission.

Wave was White Cloud's brother, so he had a strong motivation to see the conflict end peacefully. When Wave and his companion reached the Sauks' camp, the fugitives received them coolly until they realized who Wave was. Although distraught at being located so quickly, they listened to the Winnebago's message carefully. Wave reminded them of the sacredness of tobacco, and then offered the pipe to Black Hawk. The old warrior refused to smoke it, as did White Cloud and the other men. Just when Wave thought that he might fail in his mission to get the fugitives to end their hostilities, one of the boys among the fugitives took the pipe. Despite the cries of the elders not to smoke it, he put the pipe to his mouth and puffed. At that point Black Hawk's followers ended all resistance. They broke camp and followed Wave and his companion downstream to the Winnebago village.

With the smoking of the peace pipe, Black Hawk's self-appointed mission had ended. Clearly his medicine lacked power, and his effort to retain some part of the ancestral lands east of the Mississippi had failed. At the Winnebago village at La Crosse, some of the tired Sauks received a happy welcome from relatives. Black Hawk related the story of his surrender somewhat differently, suggesting that he had decided to surrender and had then traveled to the Winnebago village voluntarily. He may not have been happy having to capitulate, but he certainly did travel down the La Crosse River without coercion. Once camped at the village, he told the leaders that the Sauks had quit running. "I intended to give myself up to the American war chief, and die, if the Great Spirit saw proper," he said later. At some point in the discussion he took out his medicine bag. Using the same terms he had when encouraging the warriors before the attack on the Apple River fort, he described the medicine bundle as being "the soul of the Sauk nation." Restating his claim to have acted entirely within Sauk tradition and in an honorable fashion, he stated that the sacred object had never been dishonored in battle. "Take it, it is my life," he told the Winnebago leaders, and he asked them to give it to his captors at Prairie du Chien.

While the American authorities sought the last of the fugitive Sauks, their quarry rested at the La Crosse Winnebago village for some days in mid-August. During their stay there, the Winnebago women prepared new clothes of white deerskin for Black Hawk and White Cloud. The Indians realized the importance of pomp in their meetings with the whites and usually attended the councils dressed in their finest, so the women did what they could for the pair. When the women finished the new outfits, the two fugitive leaders donned them. Then they and their followers accompanied One Eyed Decorah and Wave to Prairie du Chien where they would surrender to Joseph Street, the resident Indian agent.

At the agency building, Street presided over the surrender ceremony. Black Hawk and White Cloud strode into the room, both clad in their new full-length white dress clothes. As the agent and the army officers watched, the two principal captives sat down. Then Decorah and Wave addressed the group. Since

Decorah was an acquaintance of Black Hawk, he knew that some of the Winnebagoes had sided with the British Band, while others had scouted or provided food and other help for the Sauk and Mesquakie people that summer. As a result, Decorah shamelessly reported having captured Black Hawk, the prophet, and the rest of the fugitives at the request of the whites: the Winnebago leaders needed all the goodwill they could generate in their dealings with the Americans that autumn because President Jackson had ordered General Scott, now in command of the mopping-up operations, to extract land from the area tribes according to their parts in the war that summer.

When the speeches ended, Street turned the prisoners over to Colonel Taylor, then commanding the troops at Fort Crawford. He kept them at the fort for several days and then ordered Lieutenant Jefferson Davis to escort the prisoners down the Mississippi to Jefferson Barracks, where they would be incarcerated until the authorities decided their fate. With many of the captives loaded aboard, the steamer *Winnebago* left Prairie du Chien and headed south. It stopped briefly at Galena on September 4, and there Black Hawk asked to speak to Street again. He claimed that he had not started the war, had even tried to prevent it, but that the chiefs had insisted on continuing north even after it had become clear that the British Band had to move back to Iowa. Because the war had not been his fault, he asked to be released in order to join Keokuk. He also promised to explain who had caused all of the trouble that summer. Nothing came of this self-serving effort.

As the steamer proceeded down the Mississippi, it stopped at the mouth of the Iowa River to release some of the captured women and children; these people then went to Keokuk's village. The other prisoners continued downriver to the Jefferson Barracks. Passing down the river past Saukenuk and other places dear to his memory, Black Hawk bemoaned his fate. In his mind's eye he saw beautiful fields now taken by the whites, a land that had belonged to the Sauks and "for which me and my people had never received a dollar.... Thus he continued his refusal to recognize the terms of the Treaty of 1804 or to believe that the annuities he and the others had taken at least up until 1818 had been in partial payment for those lands. He simply could not or would not accept the sale of Saukenuk and the nearby graveyard to the whites no matter what anyone told him.

As the *Winnebago* took Davis and his captives down the river, it avoided the towns or villages recently devastated by cholera. The prisoners reached their destination on September 7, and there they met General Atkinson, the White Beaver. Stripped of his leadership and his pride by the defeat and capture, Black Hawk felt humiliated. Soon he had other complaints, as Atkinson placed the Sauks in the guardhouse. The Indian leaders had expected incarceration, but complained when they were forced to wear leg irons too. Black Hawk again grumbled about his warrior's honor being affronted by treatment he described as "mortifying" and "useless." "Was the White Beaver afraid that I would break out of his barracks, and run away?" he asked. "Or was he ordered to inflict this punishment upon me?" Black Hawk would never have considered "wounding his feelings so much, by such treatment" had he taken Atkinson prisoner in battle. Having thus protested about wearing a ball and chain, he tempered his remarks with the comment that such treatment was a custom among the soldiers, so the General must have been doing only what he thought his duty.

While the Indian prisoners prepared to spend a gloomy winter incarcerated at Jefferson Barracks, American officials moved ahead with their plans to punish the involved tribes for the war. Beginning on September 10, 1832, General Scott and Governor Reynolds ordered the first of several councils with tribal leaders. Using agents, subagents, and interpreters, the whites addressed a series of questions to village and band leaders, among the Winnebagoes in particular. By September 12 the officials had gathered enough evidence to satisfy themselves that the Winnebagoes should pay for the wartime actions of some of its members with a land cession. After telling the Indians that the events of the past summer showed the need to separate them from the frontier

whites, Scott and Reynolds met several more times with Winnebago leaders, mostly those from the lower Wisconsin River and
the upper Rock River areas. Then on September 14 the commissioners announced a new boundary between the United States
and the Winnebago tribe—this time a boundary made by the
Great Spirit rather than the government or the Indians. The
tribe was to cede all of its lands south and east of the Fox-
Wisconsin river waterway in Wisconsin and Illinois. In return
the Indians were to get a strip of land in Iowa, some forty miles
wide and perhaps eighty miles deep, stretching west from the
Mississippi. While this might have seemed reasonable to the
American commissioners, the news must have devastated their
listeners. The proposed lands beyond the Mississippi would put
the Winnebagoes directly between the warring Sioux on the
north and the Sauks and Mesquakies on the south. Rather than
offering fine hunting, their new lands would continue to be the
scene of battles between two of the most warlike groups in the
region.

Having finished stripping the mostly innocent Winnebago
bands of much of their best land, Scott and Reynolds next
turned their attention to the hapless Sauks and Mesquakies. As-
suming that these two tribes provoked the war, the two commissioners had little choice under their orders but to extract a large
reparation in land for that action. To do that they called the village leaders from the two tribes together to meet across the river
from Fort Armstrong. There, on September 19, General Scott
stood up to speak to the chiefs. Resplendent in his full dress uni-
form and standing well over six feet tall, the general presented an
imposing figure to the fearful Indians. After reminding the tribal
leaders of the fate of Black Hawk and the prophet White Cloud
and of how well American officials had treated the captured
women and children of the tribes, Scott got down to the business at
hand. Because the British Band consisted of Sauk and Mesquakie
people and because their actions had cost the United States mil-
lions of dollars and dozens of deaths and casualties, the tribes
would have to pay for the misdeeds of their relatives.

As he had done when dealing with the Winnebagoes a week earlier, Scott suggested that one of the reasons that the Indians and pioneers had so much trouble dealing with each other resulted from their close proximity. If only the Indians lived far enough away to avoid frequent contacts with the whites, the frontier would remain more nearly at peace. To achieve that goal the United States proposed buying a strip of land at least fifty miles wide from the northern border of the Sauk and Mesquakie lands south to the Missouri River. In other words, the General called for the Indians to sell most of eastern Iowa to the United States. While demanding this land, Scott told the chiefs that the government felt entitled to it as a result of conquest and in partial payment for the costs of the war and the damages suffered by the frontier population. To show that the governments' heart was right toward the tribes, however, Scott offered an annuity of $20,000 for the next thirty years. Thus the government offered some $600,000 for something like 6,000,000 acres of some of the best land in North America.

The next day the council reassembled, and Keokuk spoke for most of the chiefs. The Indians realized the weakness of their position. If the United States wished to consider the tribes defeated enemies, they had little hope of any just settlement, so the Watchful Fox stressed the fact that the majority of both tribes had remained at peace during the Black Hawk War. Then he asked for pity on the tribes as innocent people caught up in events not of their own making. Having tried to gain some sympathy from his listeners, Keokuk then presented the Indian counterproposals. These included two reserves of land of ten square miles each, one for the Sauks and the other for the Mesquakies, at the forks of the Iowa River. Then he asked that the $1,000 perpetual annuity be cancelled and that the twenty-year annuities be increased from $20,000 to $30,000. In addition, he called for the provision of another blacksmith and gunsmith to help repair the Indians' tools and weapons, as well as forty kegs of tobacco and another forty kegs of salt each year while they received the annuities. He reminded the commissioners that when the tribes moved farther west the next year they would have no food and no prepared fields on which to raise their crop for the following year, so he asked for food and other materials to get the tribes through the transitional period.

After another day of meetings, the commissioners did something that angered and further divided the Indians. On September 21, after reading the treaty, Scott and Reynolds moved to make Keokuk the head chief of the Sauk and Mesquakie tribes. The pair claimed that the Indians themselves wished that to be done, but the officials were clearly in error. If the whites chose to choose a chief for the tribe, there was little that the Sauks or Mesquakies could do, but they neither liked nor accepted the action. Some among the tribes grumbled that although Keokuk was considered an eloquent speaker and a brave and careful war chief, nobody could make him a civil chief. One complained that "the Great Spirit only, can make a chief—i.e., a man must be born a chief, or he never can become one." However much they liked or disliked the move, the Indians signed a treaty that gave the tribes much of what Keokuk had asked for, but one that also surrendered the entire eastern portion of Iowa to the whites. Black Hawk's folly cost the Winnebagoes and the Sauks and Mesquakies large, valuable portions of their land, while making the Indians even more economically dependent upon the United States. With the so-called Black Hawk Purchase completed, American officials turned their attention to other issues, and Indian affairs in the Mississippi Valley quieted substantially.

During the negotiations with the Sauks and Mesquakies in September, General Scott had recommended that all but the ring-leaders of the British Band be released from custody and turned over to Keokuk and the civil chiefs. This had been done quickly so that only eleven men remained in custody. Those incarcerated included Black Hawk and his two sons; White Cloud, with his brother and one son; Napope; Weesheet; Ioway; Pamaho; and Chakeepashipaho, or the Little Stabbing Chief. At Jefferson Barracks the prisoners spent the long winter months bored and unhappy with their confinement. Black

Hawk remembered the winter as gloomy and described their incarceration as "not less than torture," because the Indians had
spent every other winter of their lives hunting and traveling
from one small camp to another.

Instead the captives occupied themselves making pipes and
receiving visitors. Washington Irving stopped at St. Louis in
December 1832 and made his way south of town to see the celebrated prisoners. He described them as "a forlorn crew—
emaciated and dejected," and depicted Black Hawk as "a megre
old man upwards of seventy." George Catlin, the artist, spent
some weeks trying to sketch and paint the Sauks. Generally the
Indians cooperated, but at one point Napope picked up his ball
and chain, demanding that Catlin show him wearing it. When
the artist declined to do that, the chief purposely moved around
and changed his facial expressions, making it difficult for Catlin
to get a good likeness of him. Eventually the painter did as the
Indians wished and some of his sketches do depict the prisoners
wearing their despised chains.

As the winter drew to a close, Keokuk, the civil chiefs, Davenport, and Black Hawk's wife and daughter came to visit briefly.
The Sauk tribal leaders had more than a simple visit on their
minds. They had met with Clark in St. Louis, seeking the release of the prisoners. Clark knew that the General had gotten
orders to release five of the hostages and that the others would
be taken east to a prison in Virginia where they would need less
surveillance than at Jefferson Barracks. Nevertheless, Clark
took his guests downriver aboard the steamer *Warrior* to see their
fellow tribesmen. Keokuk's visit noticeably brightened the spirits of the dejected prisoners, and they hoped that he might gain
their release. That was not to be. Instead, Clark and Atkinson
ordered the release of five of the men into the custody of the civil
chiefs, who accepted responsibility for the freedmen's future
actions. For the remaining six, however, the government had
other plans.

When he concluded the September 21, 1832 treaty with the
Sauks and Mesquakies formally ending the war, General Scott

had recommended that the government keep the captives imprisoned at Jefferson Barracks for ten years. Late that autumn, he relented, but suggested that the leaders, including Black Hawk and the prophet, be kept incarcerated. These "turbulent spirits," Scott feared, might well cause more trouble if they gained their freedom, and he saw no reason to give them any opportunity. So when the Sauk delegation asked that all of the prisoners be released in March 1833, American officials said no. Instead the government decided to send the remainder to Fortress Monroe in Virginia. "I was soon disappointed in my hopes" for a quick release from imprisonment, Black Hawk wrote. Instead of rejoining his family and friends he had to travel to Washington. He would have been even more disappointed had he known that more imprisonment lay ahead.

While the Sauk leaders and Black Hawk's wife and daughter returned to Iowa, officials at the Jefferson Barracks prepared to send their celebrated captives east. By early April they assembled the group: it included Lieutenant Thomas L. Alexander; two noncommissioned officers; the interpreter Charles St. Vrain; Black Hawk and his son Whirling Thunder, White Cloud and his adopted son; Napope; and Pamaho, a lesser leader brought along only because Weesheet was too sick to make the trip. The ten-man party set out up the Ohio River by steamboat, stopping at Louisville and Cincinnati, where large crowds of people lined the banks to see the captives. At Wheeling, Virginia, they left the river, boarded the stage, and crossed the mountains on the Cumberland Road to Frederick, Maryland. On the way their stage tipped over. Black Hawk reported that except for one of the soldiers who broke his arms, the travelers suffered no serious injuries. At Frederick the group boarded one of the earliest railroads in the country for the last leg to the capital.

In late April 1833, Lieutenant Alexander delivered his charges to War Department officials in Washington. When the Indians met President Jackson he asked them a few questions and showed them the clothes they would have to wear. Then he gave them an unpleasant surprise when he told them that they would have to live at Fortress Monroe until Indian affairs in their part of the country became quiet. The prophet protested, saying that they had not even started the war. Rather, he said, the conflict had broken out because of "our attempting to raise provisions on our own lands, or where we thought we had a right to do so." White Cloud expressed fear that their families were now exposed to attacks by the Sioux and asked the president to send them home promptly. When Jackson asked the Indians about the war, Black Hawk responded that the Indians did not expect to win because the whites had too many men. "I took up the hatchet," he said, "to revenge injuries which my people could no longer endure. Had I borne them longer without striking, my people would have said, 'Black Hawk is a woman; he is too old to be a chief; he is no Sauk.' "

Once again Black Hawk had appealed to tradition, tribal honor, and the duties of a warrior in seeking to protect what he saw as Sauk rights. His reasoning and request to be allowed to return home brought no sympathy from the president. After a tour of the Capitol, a war department armory, and other public buildings, the prisoners left Washington by stagecoach headed for Richmond. On May 1, troops escorted them to the James River, where they boarded the steamboat *Patrick Henry* for the last leg of their trip to Fort Monroe. When the tired Indians reached the fort, the officers there treated them kindly, in fact, more like guests than prisoners. Black Hawk remembered his stay in Virginia pleasantly. He commented that Colonel Abraham Eustis often stopped by to talk with them, and prior to the prisoners' release the Colonel had held a dinner in their honor.

Even while the Indians traveled between Washington and the fort, Secretary of War Lewis Cass had decided that they should be sent back to Iowa. The bedraggled prisoners were clearly tired of their incarceration and homesick. Their followers had been destroyed, and the civil chiefs of the Sauk and Mesquakie tribes seemed to have cooperated fully with American officials in the Mississippi Valley. So Cass had the Commissioner of Indian

Affairs write to Clark and Atkinson, recommending that the six men be returned quickly and placed under the civil leaders of the tribes. Both Clark and Atkinson concurred. When Cass got their replies, he ordered that the captives be released and assigned to Major John Garland for transport back to the Mississippi River and their respective tribes. To make certain that these men never caused any more trouble after they got home, Cass ordered Major Garland to take his charges west via Norfolk, Philadelphia, New York, Boston, Albany, Buffalo, and Detroit. That would take them through most of the major population centers in the East, once again employing the old line of reasoning that the number and size of the cities would impress upon the Indians the futility of any future warfare against the United States.

While in Richmond and later at Fort Monroe, the captives spent much of their time sitting for portrait artists who sketched and painted many pictures of them. While Catlin had done some of this at Jefferson Barracks, artists now kept them even busier. James Westphal Ford, a successful Virginia portrait painter, made several drawings of the captives. Others, including Charles Bird King, Samuel M. Brookes, John Wesley Jarvis, and Robert M. Sully all spent from a few days to six weeks making portraits of the men. Black Hawk failed to mention this in his autobiography, but it seems likely that he and his companions enjoyed the attention and company the artists provided. Obviously they had cooperated with this horde of artists, changing clothes frequently so that the portraits depict them in everything from their native dress to the stiff clothing of the whites.

On June 4, 1833, Major Garland led the group out of the fort and aboard the steamboat *Hampton* for their trip to Norfolk. They arrived after dark, and the next day toured the navy yard. Nothing seemed to really catch their attention until they boarded the seventy-four-gun warship *Delaware*. Although its size and armaments impressed them, the fact that the ship's figurehead was a giant Indian warrior especially pleased the visitors. Later that morning they returned to their hotel. Because the crowds kept calling for them to come out, both White Cloud and Black Hawk went out onto a balcony and through an interpreter talked to the crowd below on the street. After lunch that day they boarded the steamer *Columbus* headed for Philadelphia. Apparently the strain of their travel and the incessant crowds tired Black Hawk more than the others, and Garland took the prisoners off the boat at Baltimore because the old warrior had gotten sick. On June 6 the Indians inadvertently met President Jackson again, as both attended the same theater that evening. The next morning the president advised them to return home and remain at peace or the United States would destroy them and their people.

On June 10, Black Hawk had recovered, and the party traveled to Philadelphia, where they stayed at the Congress Hall Hotel for several days. During that time the major took them to the mint where they watched the minting process. Black Hawk later remembered that the workers had given each of them newly made coins, which he described as "very handsome." Because Major Garland's assignment was to impress his charges with the size and strength of the United States, he showed the Indians all sorts of things. The Indians visited the Philadelphia City Waterworks, the city prison, several theaters, and were even taken to a militia drill. It is unlikely that the men found much of interest at the jail, having just ended nearly a year of their own imprisonment. As for the militia, Black Hawk thought the Indian "system of military parade far better than that of the whites." The old chief also talked with Thomas L. McKenny, who had been a participant in the conduct of Indian affairs for years and was busily gathering data that would later appear in his multivolume book on Indians in the United States, published with James Hall, the writer Black Hawk had met a few years before in Illinois.

From Philadelphia, Garland moved the men on to New York City. By this time the Indians had become bored and resented being shown off to the public everywhere they went. Crowds followed them each day, and the strain of travel began to take its toll. In New York the Indians got to watch the ascent of a hot-air balloon. Astonished that the balloon really took its passenger up so high that they could barely see him or the craft, Black Hawk reported that one of the young Indians had asked the prophet if the balloonist "was going up to see the Great Spirit?" The city fathers held a large reception for the famous visitors, and one evening the prisoners enjoyed a fireworks show. But each city looked like the last one, and the ever-present crowds annoyed the travelers. Even the actress Fanny Kemble Butler, who dealt with crowds frequently, sympathized with the Indians. "That men . . . should be brought as strange animals at a show, to be gazed at the livelong day by succeeding shoals of gaping folk, struck me as totally unfitting," she wrote.

While the travelers enjoyed some of the sights, the gawking citizens impressed and intimidated the Indians, as the Indian Office officials had hoped. President Jackson had told the Indians that they would learn "that our young men are as numerous as the leaves in the woods," and asked "What can you do against us?" The large cities and immense crowds that thronged around the prisoners surely made the president's words ring true. Garland reported that "it was with difficulty that they could believe their own senses, when these populous cities and the immense crowds of people . . . were placed before their view." He felt certain that until the eastern journey these men had no idea of the size of the white population and that they had no concept of any settlement larger than St. Louis. In a speech to a Seneca chief he met in western New York, Black Hawk summed up his feelings about what he had learned from the forced visit. "Brothers, we have seen how great a people the whites are. They are very rich and very strong. It is folly for us to fight with them. We shall go home with much knowledge." Obviously neither Black Hawk nor any of his companions would ever dare risk another war with the whites after this experience.

When Garland talked of heading north to Boston, the old warrior objected. Black Hawk had trouble sleeping well, his stomach bothered him, and the incessant round of public speeches and visits had worn him down as much as General Atkinson's pursuit had the preceding summer. As a result, the major reconsidered. The president was making his way north into New England and Garland realized that Jackson had little desire to compete for public attention with the captives yet one more time, as he had done in Baltimore, Philadelphia, and New York, so the major wisely altered their plans. Instead of going up the coast to Boston, he and his companions boarded a steamer on June 22 and headed up the Hudson River to Albany. There a large crowd made it nearly impossible for the travelers to get off the boat, and in the crush of the mob a thief took Major Garland's wallet with over $100 for the trip. When the driver of the group's coach began to force his way through the unruly mob, some of the bystanders began throwing bricks, but the travelers escaped unharmed. They crossed New York State quickly, despite the complaints of the citizens along their route who wanted a better look at the Indians who had caused so much stir in the eastern press.

On June 30 the weary men boarded a lake steamer at Buffalo and began their passage through the Great Lakes. One of their fellow passengers reported that Black Hawk did not enjoy this part of his journey: he complained about the wind, and when he walked the deck he held onto his hat tightly lest it blow off into the lake; he found fault with the sleeping accommodations, too, complaining of the heat in the cabin and getting up several times during the night because he could not sleep well. Public welcomes for the Indians ended when they left Buffalo, and at Detroit the newspapers reported that a crowd hanged and burned effigies of several of the prisoners. From Detroit the party continued to Mackinac and then on to Green Bay, where they boarded a riverboat and went up the Fox River and down the Wisconsin to Prairie du Chien.

When the party reached that village, Major Garland released the prophet and his son because they lived among the Winnebagoes. Black Hawk met briefly with Street, still the Indian agent there, and recalled that "he received me very friendly." The

Sauk reminded Street that he had left his tribal medicine bag
with the Winnebago chief One Eyed Decorah when he had surrendered the previous year. Now that he was about to be released and become a free man, he said "I was anxious to get it
again, that I might hand it down to my nation unsullied!" In
their conversation the agent told him that he heard of the medicine bundle from the chiefs and that he would retrieve it and
send it to Black Hawk. Still as bitterly antiwhite as ever, the aging warrior noted that he hoped that Street would "not forget
his promise, as the whites generally do." The Winnebagoes had
reported that the agent was a good man and that he kept his
promises, so Black Hawk felt confident that he would regain his
cherished medicine bag.

From Prairie du Chien, Garland and company continued
down the Mississippi to Fort Armstrong. As they steamed down
the river, the little party passed the growing signs of white settlement on the west bank. Several hundred lead miners were working the ore deposits at Dubuque by then, to Black Hawk's
surprise. He complained that he thought President Jackson had
said that the Mississippi River was to be the boundary between
the Sauks and Mesquakies and the whites. Clearly the old warrior had misunderstood what the president had said, or perhaps
his complaints that the government's interpreter had not been
highly skilled were true. In any case, General Scott had extracted the Black Hawk Purchase from the Sauks and Mesquakies almost a year earlier, so it is little wonder that white
settlements had begun to spring up along both shores of the
river. This troubled Black Hawk because he saw the pattern of
white advance, squatting, and abuse of the Indians that he remembered from Saukenuk now beginning on the Iowa side of
the Mississippi. "I am very much afraid," he said, "that in a
few years, they will begin to drive and abuse our people, as they
have formerly done." In this case his view of the future proved to
be correct.

At Fort Armstrong, Garland reported to the commanding officer of the garrison with his prisoners and then sent messengers

out to ask the Sauk and Mesquakie leaders to meet him there. Fortunately, the Indians had just returned from a summer hunting trip and the runners met them less than twenty miles downstream. The next day the chiefs appeared with Keokuk riding under a canopy on two canoes tied together. With drums beating and warriors chanting, another twenty to thirty canoes filled with Indians paddled past the island. After that the Sauks returned to the west side of the river to finish preparing to welcome the soon-to-be-released prisoners. Later that afternoon Keokuk and his people returned to visit with Black Hawk and the others. After some talk and pipe smoking, Keokuk and the others left. The next day at midmorning they returned to the room set aside for the council meeting at the fort. With Keokuk and Pashipaho on one side and Wapello, the Mesquakie leader, on the other, the Indians waited for Black Hawk and his companions to appear. Both Black Hawk and his son had objected to the council as unnecessary; they wanted to return to the tribe and hoped to avoid being publicly humiliated by having to submit to Keokuk and the civil chiefs, but the whites insisted on the council. After Major Garland gave a brief welcoming talk, Keokuk welcomed the prisoners back to the tribe.

Then, just to make certain that everyone understood the president's wishes, Garland spoke again. This time his words, as the interpreter rendered them, angered the old warrior deeply. He understood the major to say that Black Hawk was to "follow Keokuk's advice and be governed by his council in all things." Black Hawk complained that Garland's talk included things he found insulting. Black Hawk stood quickly, so angry that he trembled as he spoke; saying that he was an old man, he continued "I will act for myself; no one shall govern me." As he sat down amidst the surprised talk of the other Indians, he realized his mistake. If he refused to obey Keokuk, the government might not release him to the tribe. Before he could say more, Keokuk rose, chiding him in Sauk and then apologized for the outburst. Later, when Black Hawk regained his composure, he spoke in more moderate terms, and Garland agreed to his release the next day. Despite the softer words to the officer, the old Sauk still resented the major's words and tone. Later he labeled Garland's speech as uncalled for and unbecoming, and recalled that he had never had his "feelings of pride and honor insulted" as badly as they had been on this occasion. That same evening the officers at the fort held a small party for the now-freed prisoners and the visiting chiefs. They exchanged pipes and then sampled some champagne, which the Indians apparently tried for the first time. With good feelings evident, the officers and the Indians all said pleasant things, and even Black Hawk seemed gracious for a change. He thanked the tribal leaders for caring for his wife and daughter, invited Major Garland and several others to visit his lodge, and shook hands. With that the ceremonies ended, and the next morning Keokuk and the others crossed the Mississippi into Iowa, taking the last four members of the British Band with them.

With his wife, daughter, and two sons nearby, Black Hawk settled near Keokuk's village on the Iowa River. In 1833 at Rock Island, Black Hawk dictated an account of his life to the interpreter LeClair and a young newspaperman, J. P. Patterson, who edited and published it later that same year. The next year the Reverend Cutting Marsh, a Presbyterian missionary visiting from Wisconsin, described the old man's lodge as a "specimine of neatness and good order," one of the few positive things he reported about the Sauks that summer. Two years later at a council between the Sauks and Mesquakies and the United States, the artist George Catlin saw Black Hawk again. He characterized the old man as a "poor dethroned monarch," and "an object of pity." While the meeting occurred, Catlin reported that Black Hawk "with an old frock coat and a brown hat on, and a cane in his hand," stood outside the main group "in dumb and dismal silence...." In 1837 when tribal business called for another trip to Washington, Keokuk and the other chiefs took the aging warrior along, probably just to keep him from getting into trouble while they were gone. While in the East this second time, Black Hawk attracted much less attention than he had in 1833, but he did pose for Charles Bird King again.

Back in Iowa the old man got along well with his white neighbors. In 1838 he had moved to a new home on the Des Moines River, and soon after that the local citizens invited him to their Fourth of July celebration at Fort Madison. After several toasts the master of ceremonies asked Black Hawk to respond and he did, praising the local country as rich and bountiful. He told the audience that he had loved his country and fought for it. Now he urged the new owners to keep it beautiful. As he concluded his brief remarks, Black Hawk returned to a theme that ran through much of his life. "I was once a great warrior," he said. "Now I am poor. Keokuk has been the cause of my present situation. . . . " On October 3, 1838, at the age of seventy-two, Black Hawk died after a short illness. Less than a year later a local doctor stole the corpse and took it to St. Louis, where he had the bones cleaned and wired together. When Iowa governor Robert Lucas learned of this, he recovered the skeleton and had it deposited in the Burlington Geological and Historical Society: Black Hawk's last remains perished in 1855 when fire destroyed that building.

Black Hawk's life had stretched from an era that predated the founding of the United States as an independent nation to the destruction and removal of the Indians east of the Mississippi. His pride in Sauk culture, personal attachment to the village of Saukenuk, concern that the tribal medicine bundle not be dishonored, and outlook as a warrior all represented the ideals of previous generations. Even by the era of his birth the Sauks had already been forced to migrate repeatedly because of the invasion of North America by the Europeans. While many traditional social, economic, and political practices continued well into Black Hawk's lifetime, the Sauk culture and economy had been unalterably changed by the impact of the fur trade, European diseases, and increased intertribal warfare. As a result, the traditions that Black Hawk represented no longer sufficed, they offered an uncertain future. That is not to say that Black

Hawk's traditional beliefs may not have represented everything good and honorable in Sauk life, but only to note that the changed situation called for courses of action that no longer led down the warrior's path. Black Hawk's negative judgments of Keokuk as ignoble, self-seeking, and even cowardly appear well founded, given the old warrior's traditional world view.

Clearly the Watchful Fox did not live up to the Sauk ideal of a tribal war leader. Nevertheless, Keokuk had been east to Washington: he knew of the size of the United States and the numbers of its people; he realized that against a people so numerous that the Sauks had no chance to prevail, so he chose the more difficult road—that of negotiation and adaptation. In the long run Keokuk's approach brought no more success than did the proud resistance led by Black Hawk. The onslaught of white society proved to be just as destructive to the Sauk and Mesquakie peoples after 1832 as the guns of General Atkinson's soldiers had been during the campaign that destroyed the British Band. So the old warrior's insistence on living by the standards of the past may have made sense culturally at the time. If cooperation and accommodation brought degradation and near destruction, what was lost through warfare and overwhelming defeat?

And what of Black Hawk the man? He proved a dynamic leader at an age when most men of his era were either dead or retired. As a tactician and a military leader he had often received considerable praise from the American officers involved in the campaigns against him. In public debate with excellent speakers such as Keokuk, his skills foundered, yet when it came time to call out the warriors or to inspire his followers, Black Hawk had succeeded repeatedly. While his attitudes reflected the dictates of earlier generations, he remained true to them. Black Hawk saw his life as having been spent working for the defense of the Sauk nation, for the retention of their traditional eighteenth-century lands, and for tribal honor. He often said that Sauk military actions all stemmed from the need to protect the villagers or to respond to injuries, deaths, or damage inflicted on the tribe by its enemies. His assessment of Sauk participation in the War of 1812 demonstrated that understanding of the situation. When the United States failed to live up to its reputed promises of available credit and good trade goods, he said that the Indians had no choice but to join the British in order to get the trade goods they needed to survive the 1812 winter. After Stillman's forces fired on his men bearing a white flag, he again claimed that there was no choice but to go to war, one forced on him by white treachery.

Even if Black Hawk's view offered an accurate understanding of the tribal situation during his lifetime, his actions were less than consistent and not always entirely honorable. A proud, stubborn man, Black Hawk had trouble taking advice or directions unless they agreed with his conservative views. Because of his intense personal identification with the Sauk tribe and its well-being, those who offered alternative courses of action often found him uncooperative, even unyielding. Along with being stubborn, he had a strong temper which got him into difficulties. His repeated outbursts when agents, interpreters, army officers, or traders suggested that the tribe had actually sold its lands to the government or that the Indians would have to vacate Saukenuk, indicate that upon hearing unpleasant or unwanted news Black Hawk reacted badly and often without careful thought.

Because he remained persuaded that he knew best for the Sauks, Black Hawk not only refused to consider alternatives to his position, but, worse, also allowed himself to believe stories that had no basis in fact. In some ways he was as naive as a small child, engaging in the most blatant wishful thinking and refusing to ask critical questions of those who misled him. Even during early April 1832, when all the evidence he saw each day told him that no other tribes would help the British Band, Black Hawk insisted on continuing up the Rock River. Although fully persuaded that no other help was coming and that Napope and the prophet had lied to him, he actively tried to hide that knowledge from the average members of the group, even meeting secretly with visiting delegations of chiefs so that the bad news would not spread and ruin the morale of the people.

The old warrior found it difficult to admit making mistakes or taking bad advice. When his actions proved to be devastating, he hid behind the excuse that he was only a war leader and not a chief. For example, Black Hawk declared petulantly that General Atkinson should ask the chiefs and not him about the motives of the British Band, even though he, not they, had led the group. His insistence that the whites had lied to the Sauks every time they had put things on paper helped to poison the tribe's relations with American officials for several decades. Occasionally Black Hawk would acknowledge the honor or truthfulness of a particular white official, but more often than not he included all of them in his blanket denunciations.

Because Black Hawk believed that others made the mistakes, lied to him, cheated the tribe repeatedly, and generally could not be trusted, Black Hawk's actions seem more understandable and defensible than they might otherwise be. Certainly some of his reluctance to accept the restraints of tribal leaders resulted from their elevation of Keokuk to the position of War Chief during the War of 1812 while Black Hawk had been off fighting as an ally of the British. The relationship between these two proud, able men suffered or remained difficult much of the time because of that. If the whites really lied when they negotiated agreements or when they got the tribal leaders to sign papers, then the proud warrior's reluctance to honor the chiefs is understandable. Black Hawk felt that the chiefs had allowed themselves to be duped and had shown bad judgment and failed to deserve the honor or obedience shown to them by the rest of the tribe. His willingness to accept the urgings of the Winnebago prophet might have been a traditional response to new and troubling conditions. It might also have been mere wish fulfillment because the situation of the Sauks had become more desperate each year.

Black Hawk's life demonstrates that leaders base their actions on many things: his strong traditional beliefs and practices shaped his outlook toward major issues in a rapidly changing situation; his belief that only the Indians dealt with others honorably tainted his relations with the whites; his insistence that his way was not only the best approach to the Sauk's problems but the only patriotic way to do things disrupted relations with other leaders within the tribe. Black Hawk's unyielding personality, pride in personal accomplishments and position, and leadership skills all made him a formidable leader and a person who could not be ignored: at the same time few could work with him for any length of time without having some disagreements. Throughout his life Black Hawk thought of himself as a patriotic Sauk, a warrior first and foremost, yet his ideals and beliefs belonged to an earlier, simpler era: one during which the Sauk people could live in traditional ways, free from major interference by the United States. During the early nineteenth century that freedom disappeared abruptly, leaving the Indians with few guidelines to follow. Some chose to bend with the times. Others, such as Black Hawk, resisted. Unfortunately, by the time Black Hawk had reached mature adulthood, the once-honored warrior's path led only to defeat, not to solutions that might have helped his people survive.

BIBLIOGRAPHICAL ESSAY

Writing the biography of an Indian leader, dead more than 150 years now, is something like trying to catch the shadows of clouds as they cross the beach on a warm summer afternoon. It is difficult and frustrating work at best. Still a surprising number and variety of sources remain that proved useful for this study. Few Native Americans knew English well during the early nineteenth century, and fewer still left any written documents for later use by scholars. Because not many of the tribal languages had been put to paper at the time, little information is available to give insights into the Indian side of the story. In Black Hawk's case, however, he dictated a memoir of his life that is crucial for understanding his ideas about what happened. Interestingly enough, it appeared before any of the professional writers or participants in the 1832 war got around to telling their versions of the story.

According to Antoine LeClaire, the interpreter at Rock Island, shortly after he returned to Iowa in August 1833, Black Hawk approached him with the idea of telling his life story. It is possible that some of the people the old warrior met while on his eastern tour suggested the idea to him, or even that LeClaire and the editor John B. Patterson asked him to participate in the venture. In any event, Patterson, who published the *Galenian*, a newspaper in Galena during the 1832 war, was largely responsible for the final form in which the Sauk leader's story reached the public. LeClaire, while a thoroughly competent interpreter, did not speak English as his first language, so Patterson took what the Frenchman gave him and put it into a more acceptable literary form. The resulting book, *Life of Ma-Ka-Tia-Me-She-Kia-Kiak or*

Black Hawk (Cincinnati: J. B. Patterson, 1833), then, represents Black Hawk's ideas strained through LeClaire's interpretation and shaped by Patterson's editorial ideas and skills.

Because of the editor's ideas about proper nineteenth-century literary style, the account includes what seems to be silly phraseology at times. At other times, Black Hawk's narrative skips around and his chronology is confused at best. Without doubt, he gives a biased and self-serving defense of his own actions throughout the narrative. Despite these obvious flaws, the account rings true. The text includes data that neither the translator nor the editor could have known prior to the 1833 publication of the book. In addition, the outlook, ideas, and depth of feeling that are found throughout the narrative mark it as genuine beyond all question. Therefore, even with its flaws and gaps, Black Hawk's autobiography is invaluable for any serious effort to understand Sauk customs and ideas during the early nineteenth century, and even more so for explaining his own motivations and actions.

Several scholars have discussed the autobiography's strengths and weaknesses at length. In the introduction of his 1955 edition of *Black Hawk: An Autobiography* (Urbana: University of Illinois Press) Donald Jackson traces discussions of its genesis and accuracy from early reviews in 1835 down to the time of his study. While admitting that questions remain about how much of the final version of the book came from the Indian and how much came from the editor, Jackson provides evidence to convince all but the most determinedly skeptical that it is an acceptable source for a study of the Sauk leader. In his essay "Black Hawk: A Reassessment," *Annals of Iowa* 45 (Spring, 1981):599–619, John E. Hallwas points out clearly how the Indian leader's attitudes and ideas may be extracted from the autobiography and the copies of his few public statements. Arnold Krupat, in *For Those Who Came After: Indian Autobiography: Origins, Type, and Function* (Berkeley: University of California Press, 1985) describes and evaluates the intermixture of Indian narrator, mixed-blood interpreter, and white editor in creating the autobiography.

Black Hawk's life and the war that carries his name have received considerable attention almost from his day to the present. After his own autobiography appeared in several editions during the 1830s, other accounts of his life found their way into print. In 1838, the year the Indian leader died, Benjamin Drake published the first of several versions of *The Life and Adventures of Black Hawk* (Cincinnati: George Conclin, 1838). Drake talked to many of the participants in the 1832 war and to others who knew or had dealt with the old Sauk, and his account is surprisingly positive for its time. Other figures of that day published accounts too. John A. Wakefield's *History of the War Between the United States and the Sac and Fox Nations of Indians* (Jacksonville, Ill.: C. Goudy, 1834) gives an accurate account of the 1832 war from a militiaman's view. Although strongly anti-Indian, it is factually accurate. Ninian Edwards, Illinois governor during the late 1820s, has his side of the events told by his son, Ninian Wirt Edwards, in *History of Illinois from 1778 to 1833; and Life and Times of Ninian Edwards* (Springfield: The Illinois State Journal Company, 1870). Governor John Reynolds gave a highly critical account of all the Indians in his state in his *Reynolds' History of Illinois, My Own Times: Embracing also the History of My Life* (Chicago: Chicago Historical Society, 1879).

Historical studies of Black Hawk's life and the Black Hawk War give no consensus about these events. Rather they shift from a pro-Indian stance to an anti-Indian one and back while occasionally pronouncing a plague on both sides. The most pro-Indian account is Perry A. Armstrong's *The Sauks and the Black Hawk War* (Springfield, Illinois: H. W. Rooker, 1887). Repeatedly Armstrong found fault with the whites and praised the Indians. In its own way, Armstrong's history is as biased and one-sided as Governor Reynolds's early discussion. In *The Black Hawk War, Including a Review of Black Hawk's Life* (Chicago: Frank E. Stevens, 1903), Frank E. Stevens gives a detailed and carefully prepared discussion. Determined to portray the Indian warrior as evil, dishonest, or just wrong-headed, Stevens swings the pendulum back to the anti-Indian approach. Several decades later Cyrenus Cole, in his *I Am a Man. The Indian Black Hawk* (Iowa City: State Historical Society of Iowa, 1938), tried to treat the subject even-handedly, but his work includes some incorrect material and adds little to the earlier accounts.

Modern treatments make better use of ethnohistorical data, but even they demonstrate a wide variation in assessing the events under consideration. William T. Hagan's *The Sac and Fox Indians* (Norman: University of Oklahoma Press, 1958) began as a study of the 1832 war, but he expanded it to focus on the first half of the nineteenth century. Hagan noted errors in judgment by government officials, Indian leaders, and the pioneers and spread the blame for the problems to all three groups. He gives the best discussion of the 1800–32 events available and places the issues within the broad context of early nineteenth-century American territorial expansion. Anthony F. C. Wallace's "Prelude to Disaster: The Course of Indian-White Relations Which Led to the Black Hawk War of 1832," Vol. 1, pp. 1–51, in Ellen M. Whitney, ed., *The Black Hawk War 1831–32*, focuses carefully on the Indian motivations and understanding of the 1804–1832 era.

As the Vietnam War came to an end, the antimilitary feelings of that era led Cecil Eby to write *"That Disgraceful Affair," The Black Hawk War* (New York: W. W. Norton, 1973). Here the author traces the actions of all the participants carefully, but has difficulty getting away from his strong antiwar feelings. As a result he seems unable to separate understandable motivations from the stupid mistakes of the leading figures and therefore adds little to the existing knowledge of this white-Indian conflict. The most recent study of the upper Mississippi Valley situation is Allan W. Eckert's *Twilight of Empire, A Narrative* (Boston: Little, Brown, and Company, 1988). This book discusses the events in Black Hawk's life in a thoroughly uncritical manner. It includes dialogue for which there is no record and is the least reliable account of these events.

Manuscript and archival materials dealing with certain aspects of Black Hawk's life abound. As might be expected the midwestern state historical societies have most of the pertinent items. The Draper manuscript collection, now available on microfilm from the State Historical Society of Wisconsin, includes the Thomas Forsyth correspondence. The agent at Rock Island from 1818 until 1830, Forsyth's letters are crucial. In addition, the Madison facility has the papers of Joseph M. Street, agent at Prairie du Chien, as well as collections of material from Nicholas Boilvin, Thomas F. Burnett, and William Henry Harrison. It also has microfilmed copies of the papers of Andrew Jackson and Zachary Taylor.

The Illinois State Historical Library in Springfield has the invaluable Black Hawk War collection as well as the Frank E. Stevens papers, gathered while he worked on his history of the Black Hawk War. The papers of other important individuals who participated in these events are scattered in several libraries. William Clark materials are housed at the Missouri Historical Society in St. Louis as well as at the Kansas State Historical Society in Topeka. The latter collection is available on microfilm. The Missouri Historical Society also houses material belonging to Thomas Forsyth, the Choteau family of fur traders in Missouri, and a collection known as the Indian Papers.

The federal officials, both military and civil, who dealt with the Sauks, Mesquakies, and their tribal neighbors kept voluminous records, and their correspondence is available at the National Archives. Several collections contain most of the significant material. These include Record Group 75, Records of the Office of Indian Affairs; Record Group 107, Records of the Office of the Secretary of War; Record Group 94, Records of the Office of the Adjutant General; and Record Group 108, Records of the Headquarters of the Army. The most useful items are found in Record Group 75, Records of the Office of Indian Affairs. These include Letters Sent, 1824–38; Letters Received, 1824–38; Prairie du Chien Agency; Rock Island Agency; and St. Louis Superintendency.

Because English traders and British officials had frequent meetings with the tribes within the United States, material in

Canada provides that side of the relationship. The archives at the Fort Malden National Historic Park include material on British-Indian dealings for the 1800–15 era. The Public Archives of Canada have considerable holdings too. In their collections, Manuscript Group 19 contains the family and personal papers of William Claus and the McKees, who dealt with the American tribes. The largest collection of material is found in Record Group 10 of the Indian Department. Among the published accounts of British materials, see "Papers from the Canadian Archives," *Wisconsin Historical Collections* Vol. 12 (Madison: State Historical Society of Wisconsin, 1892):23–132; and the "Papers of Thomas G. Anderson, British Indian Agent, 1814–1821," *Wisconsin Historical Collections* Vol. 10 (Madison: State Historical Society of Wisconsin, 1885): 142–49.

Much of the American documentary material has also been published. The federal government began the process during the 1830s and has continued to provide material ever since. The most applicable items may be found in the *American State Papers: Indian Affairs*, 2 vols. (Washington, D.C.: Gales and Seaton, 1832–34), and *American State Papers: Military Affairs*, 7 vols. (Washington, D.C.: Gales and Seaton, 1832–61). These two sets include reports from Indian agents, treaty negotiators, and military discussions. The government also published *The Territorial Papers of the United States*, 27 vols. (Washington, D.C.: GPO, 1934–70), edited by Clarence E. Carter and John Porter Bloom. These volumes focus on major issues within each particular territory, and the most pertinent are those on Indiana, Illinois, Missouri, and Michigan. They include many items from the National Archives that would otherwise be unavailable without a trip to Washington, and are extraordinarily well annotated and indexed.

The midwestern state historical societies and libraries have published many items of interest too. In 1922 the Indiana Historical Commission published a two-volume set of documents as Volumes 7 and 9 of the *Indiana Historical Collections*, edited by Logan Esary and entitled *Governor's Messages and Letters: Messages and*

Letters of William Henry Harrison (Indianapolis, 1922). This material is also available in a reprinted edition published by Arno Press (New York, 1975). *The Wisconsin Historical Collections*, published by the State Historical Society of Wisconsin, includes published documents, reminiscent accounts, and article-length items that focus on the 1750–1840 era, as do the *Collections of the Michigan Pioneer and Historical Society* and the *Collections of the Illinois State Historical Library*. By far the single most valuable published collection is that compiled and edited by Ellen M. Whitney. Entitled *The Black Hawk War 1831–1832*, this was published as volumes *35–38* of the *Collections of the Illinois State Historical Library* (Springfield, 1970–1978). This is an excellent collection, and no study of midwestern tribal affairs that includes the Sauks and Mesquakies can overlook it.

Specific studies of Sauk and Mesquakie cultures include: M. R. Harrington, "Sacred Bundles of the Sac and Fox Indians," *University of Pennsylvania Anthropological Publications*, Vol. 4 (1914); Frederick W. Hodge, ed., *Handbook of American Indians North of Mexico*, Bureau of American Ethnology, *Bulletin No.* 30, 2 vols. (Washington, D.C.: GPO, 1907); William Jones, *Ethnography of the Fox Indians*, Bureau of American Ethnology, *Bulletin No.* 125, 2 vols. (Washington, D.C.: GPO, 1939); Alanson Skinner, *Observations on the Ethnology of the Sauk Indians*, Public Museum of Milwaukee, *Bulletin No.* 5 (Milwaukee, Wis., 1823–25); Zachary Gussow and Raleigh Barlowe, *Sac, Fox, and Iowa Indians* (New York: Garland Publishing Co., 1974); Charles Callender, "Fox," in Bruce G. Trigger, ed., *Handbook of North American Indians: Northeast* (Washington, D.C.: GPO, 1978), 15:636–47; and Callender, "Sauk," in Trigger, Handbook, 15:648–55.

Other items that consider related issues include: Melvin L. Fowler and Robert L. Hall, "Late Prehistory of the Illinois Area," in Trigger, *Handbook*, 15:560–68; J. Josephy Bauxar, "History of the Illinois Area," in Trigger, *Handbook*, 15:594–601; Charles Callender, "Great Lakes-Riverine Sociopolitical Organization," in Trigger, *Handbook*, 15:610–21; David Stout, Erminie Wheeler-Voegelin, and Emily J. Blasingham, *Indians of Eastern Missouri*,

Western Illinois, and Southern Wisconsin From the Proto-Historic Period to 1804 (New York: Garland Publishing Co., 1974); and Charles Callender, *Social Organization of the Central Algonkian Indians*, Public Museum of Milwaukee, *Publication in Anthropology, No.* 7 (Milwaukee, Wis., 1962). For a general discussion of the impact of European trade goods on the tribes see George I. Quimby's *Indian Culture and European Trade Goods: The Archaeology of the Historical Period in the Western Great Lakes Region* (Madison: University of Wisconsin Press, 1977). To gain an understanding of tribal migrations and the shifting of village sites, see Helen Hornbeck Tanner, ed., *Atlas of Great Lakes Indian History* (Norman: University of Oklahoma Press, 1986).

Other nearby tribes have also received considerable attention, and their experiences offer a good background against which to consider what happened to the Sauks and Mesquakies. R. David Edmunds has three books that deal with some of the same issues discussed here. They are *The Potawatomis: Keepers of the Fire* (Norman: University of Oklahoma Press, 1978); *The Shawnee Prophet* (Lincoln: University of Nebraska Press, 1983); and *Tecumseh and the Quest for Indian Leadership* (Boston: Little, Brown and Company, 1984). For other midwestern tribes, see Arrell M. Gibson's *The Kickapoos: Lords of the Middle Border* (Norman: University of Oklahoma Press, 1963); Bert Anson's *The Miami Indians* (Norman: University of Oklahoma Press, 1970); Harvey L. Carter's *Little Turtle* (Urbana: University of Illinois Press, 1987); and John J. Mathews's *The Osages: Children of the Middle Waters* (Norman: University of Oklahoma Press, 1961). For a general discussion of tribal activities during the seventeenth century see W. Vernon Kinietz's *The Indians of the Western Great Lakes,* 1615–1750 (Ann Arbor: University of Michigan Press, 1965).

In the process of American territorial expansion that led to most of the conflict with the Indians, British authorities worked with the tribes. The contrasts between how the two governments dealt with the tribal people is an important part of the story. Reginald Horsman's *Expansion and American Indian Policy,* 1783–1812

(East Lansing: Michigan State University Press, 1967) provides a solid base for understanding the basic issues. His *Matthew Elliott: British Indian Agent* (Detroit: Wayne State University Press, 1964) gives a detailed look at part of the story. For a view focused on the Mississippi Valley rather than on the Great Lakes region, see Kate L. Gregg's "The War of 1812 on the Missouri Frontier," *Missouri Historical Review* 33 (October, 1938):3–22; (January, 1939):184–202 and (April, 1939):326–48. Her account provides considerable material not found elsewhere. The most even-handed study of the War of 1812 that gives Indian affairs primary consideration is Alec R. Gilpin's *The War of 1812 in the Old Northwest* (East Lansing: Michigan State University Press, 1958). For other aspects of American-Indian military relations during the early nineteenth century, see Roger L. Nichols's *General Henry Atkinson: A Western Military Career* (Norman: University of Oklahoma Press, 1965); and Francis P. Prucha's *Sword of the Republic: The United States Army on the Frontier, 1783–1846* (New York: Macmillan Co., 1969), and *A Guide to the Military Posts of the United States* (Madison: State Historical Society of Wisconsin, 1964).

To gain a general understanding of relations between the United States and the Sauks see the first volume of Francis P. Prucha's *The Great Father: The United States Government and the Indians*, 2 vols. (Lincoln: University of Nebraska Press, 1984). This gives a detailed look at the development of national policies. One might also use Ronald D. Satz's *American Indian Policy in the Jacksonian Era* (Lincoln: University of Nebraska Press, 1977). William T. Hagan's previously mentioned *The Sac and Fox Indians* places the tribes of the upper Mississippi Valley into the general patterns of Indian policy. For specific treaty provisions dealing with each tribe, see William H. Kappler, ed., *Indian Affairs: Laws and Treaties*, 2 vols. (Washington, D.C.: GPO, 1899–1900) or the more recent five-volume edition of this material. To see how the treaties worked out on the ground, see Charles C. Royce, compiler, *Indian Land Cessions in the United States*, Bureau of American Ethnology, Report No. 18, part 2 (Washington, D.C.: GPO, 1904).

INDEX

Black Hawk and the Warrior's Path was copyedited and proofread by Andrew J. Davidson. Production editor was Lucy Herz. The text was typeset by Point West, Inc., and printed and bound by McNaughton & Gunn.

Book design by Roger Eggers.